MAKING FRIENDS

Biography

Anita M Hughes BA MEd CPsychol AFBPsS is a teacher and chartered educational psychologist. She worked in social services and education services in South Wales, London and Surrey before setting up in private practice in 1999 in Guildford, Surrey.

When Anita worked as a consultant in the council day nurseries of Hammersmith & Fulham in the early 1980s she met and worked with Elinor Goldschmied, collaborating in writing, teaching and film making and developing the ideas of Heuristic Play. Anita has also published three books about play and learning in the Early Years as well as collaborating with Veronica Read in a book for teachers on how to build positive relationships with parents.

On moving to Surrey in 1986, Anita began working in local authority mainstream and special schools across the age range. She worked with teachers and parents to assess children's learning, emotional and behavioural difficulties and to support them through classroom advice, running groups and training courses. It was at this time that her interest in autism developed into a passion and she started to run groups for children in schools, together with teaching support staff to run their own groups.

Anita set up the Friendly Group in 1999 when she began her own private practice. Her private practice has included IQ assessments, consultation advice, counselling and delivering training workshops. In recent years her focus has been on family and individual counselling. However, her overriding love is her work with ASD children, young people and their parents.

MAKING FRIENDS

How the Friendly Group supports children and young people on the Autism Spectrum

Anita M Hughes

STORIES OF CONNECTION AND HOPE

Worth Publishing
worthpublishing.com

First published 2017 by Worth Publishing Ltd
worthpublishing.com
© Worth Publishing Ltd 2017

All rights reserved. No part of this publication may be reproduced, stored in a retrieval system or transmitted in any form, or by any means, electronic, mechanical, photocopying, recording or otherwise, without the prior permission of the publishers, nor be otherwise circulated without the publisher's consent in any form of binding or cover other than that in which it is published and without a similar condition being imposed on the subsequent purchaser.

Printed and bound in Great Britain by TJ International, Padstow, Cornwall

British Library Cataloguing in Publication Data

A catalogue record for this book is available from the British Library

ISBN   ISBN 9781903269381

Cover and text design by Anna Murphy

Dedicated to Sara and Mark
who made sure the Friendly Group started
and to all the children who followed thereafter.

In memory of my darling friend and assistant
Hayley Hazelby (*1984 - 2013*),
who loved the Friendly Group children
and is sorely missed.

Acknowledgements

This book has been written with love and gratitude to all the Friendly Group families who have inspired me over the years and who have encouraged me to tell their children's stories.

To my dear friend and colleague Tess Miller, who started the Friendly Group with me and encouraged me to write, I say a big thank you. I would also like to thank my many Friendly Group colleagues - Jo Neate, Claire Bullen, Gaby Alexander, Vicky Clancy, Zaynab Alfadhl, Jan Walker, Lucy Nathanson, Janet Paterson, Marisa Ciesla, Angela Davies, Libby Hughes, Johnny Maher and Thomas Wilkins - for their wonderful assistance, care and attention in running the groups and helping me to examine and question the way I work.

There are countless other friends who have helped me along the way to have faith and to keep going when I doubted myself - Peter Danby, Sarah Rozenthuler, Chrissie Astell, Chris Frampton, Andrew Woodgate, Diane Sylvester, Dereca Trevail, Jeannette Walker and Barbara Robinson. I express deep gratitude to all of you for being there when I needed you.

Above all I want to express my deepest appreciation and thanks to two very special people in my life; my husband Graham and my friend and mentor Ewa Gottesman. Graham has patiently listened to me and encouraged me. He has read and re-read my drafts over many years and allowed me countless hours of privacy and quiet in which to think and write. Ewa has not only taught me about group therapy, she believed in me when I doubted myself and encouraged me when I faltered. She meticulously read every word, commenting on my style till I 'found my voice'. She has patiently listened to me and generously and unfailingly shared her wisdom, knowledge and kindness over the past eight years. This book would have never been written without her.

Finally I would like to thank my enthusiastic and supportive publishing editor, Andrea Perry, for sowing the seeds of the book ten years ago, then patiently attending to every detail of my writing along the way; putting up with delays and doubts and ensuring that the book 'emerged in its own time'.

Hope

> Hope is a state of mind, not of the world. Hope, in this deep and powerful sense, is not the same as joy that things are going well, or willingness to invest in enterprises that are obviously heading for success, but rather an ability to work for something because it is good. The more propitious the situation in which we demonstrate hope, the deeper the hope is…
>
> Hope is definitely not the same thing as optimism. It is not the conviction that something will turn out well, but the certainty that something makes sense, regardless of how it turns out.
>
> The hope of the world lies in the rehabilitation of the living human being, not just the body but also the soul.
>
> Quotes from Vaclav Havel (first president of the Czech Republic)

Contents

	Introduction	1
1	It often starts like this	9
2	Autism Spectrum Disorder, Asperger's Syndrome and Attachment	19
3	Preparation for the Friendly Group: a family commitment	45
4	The session framework - the six rhythms	61
5	Circle Time with the stone	73
6	Group process: working in the here-and-now	81
7	The leadership role	93
8	Tension and turbulence	99
9	The Worry Bear and sensory issues	111
10	The trolley and the trampoline	121

(continues ...)

Contents (continued)

11	Imagination: the story and the obstacle course	**139**
12	I can't say what I feel	**153**
13	The issue of bullying and the opportunity for growth	**173**
14	Stuck in transition	**193**
15	The Café Group	**205**
16	Cancer calls: Christpher's story	**225**
17	Beginnings in endings	**241**
	Appendix	**255**
	References and further reading	**257**

Introduction

On his journey to meet me for the first time, ten-year-old Steve asked his mother for more information about the Friendly Group. How do people make friends? How do you learn to do it? How can a group learn to make friends if no-one is very good at it?

Steve was an only child. He had never had what we might call a good friend. He thought he had friends because he ran around in the playground alongside other children. What he hadn't experienced was what it feels like to be in an ongoing relationship with someone of his own age; sharing secrets, taking risks together, telling jokes and being prepared to compromise in games. If he did try to play a game it fell apart, because he always wanted other children to play by and keep to his rules. In essence, he was lonely and awkward: but he hadn't ever known anything else.

Steve asked good questions and made a good point. In any group at any one time there need to be some members who find it easier to make relationships, so they can support others who might be struggling. What Steve didn't know is that the Friendly Group is what is known as a 'slow-open' group (Grotjahn, 1993). This means that a group is never comprised of children who are all completely 'new'. There will always be a core of children who have attended the group for some time.

In Steve's case, he was the only new member. He was joining a group of children and young people who already had some experience of what it feels like to begin to make friendships, however clumsily. More importantly, the other children already had experience of learning to trust that the group was a safe place to try 'reaching out' to others, expressing feelings without fear of being laughed at, unwittingly led on or needing to make a sudden escape from an overwhelming situation. It was also a place where the upsets and misunderstandings that happen in play and social interaction are not experienced as '*the end of the world*', but can be '*sorted out*' by the children themselves, and no-one is in the wrong. Indeed it is often the misunderstandings and upsets that provide those very moments which offer the best opportunity for growth and self discovery.

It's also in those moments that the sensitivity, clarity, emotional strength and good timing of the group leaders come in to play. The adults need to demonstrate that they are calm, confident and are standing firm to 'hold' the emotions of the child or children in distress, just as a mother might with her crying infant.

When I met Steve I immediately liked him. He was curious and bubbled with enthusiasm and wanted to give the Friendly Group a try. I liked the key questions he posed because they have been asked of me over the years, by professionals and parents alike. How can children with difficulties in social communication learn from each other? Where are the role models, if they all have problems? How can children and young people on the autism spectrum learn about empathy; about being able to imagine how someone else is feeling or thinking or might behave?

It was these questions that prompted me to write this book. I wanted to be able to explore how groups can work and help youngsters with autism and Autistic Spectrum Disorder, and to share my thoughts and discoveries. The children and young people I've worked with have been my greatest teachers, and continue to be. The Friendly Group has evolved out of practices and rhythms that seem to work, but has also been based on sound psychological and group analytical principles from the start. It is not the only way to work in a group, but it has worked for me and my colleagues. It is my hope that by learning about this particular group, others might feel inspired to start their own along similar principles.

Containment and removing the obstacles to growth

It is hard to imagine how bewildering it must feel to be a child or teenager who wants to make friends and do things with others, yet doesn't know how to make social connections and satisfying relationships without being overwhelmed by unpredictable feelings of anxiety and frustration. Such overwhelming feelings trigger behaviours that create isolation and disconnection.

All children, indeed all of us, know what it feels like to be confused and anxious. When anxiety levels get too high, we can't think properly. As we go through childhood, most of us develop the capacity to think about feelings and tolerate frustration. Just the act of thinking about and expressing feelings can make them more understandable and manageable. Furthermore, when feelings and frustrations are expressed towards someone whom we trust, this 'contains' the feelings and we feel better. If that other person acknowledges the difficult feelings with something like, *"I understand how you feel"*, or *"I can see you are upset"*, we might sigh with the relief of being understood, and can then think more clearly again. It was Wilfred Bion, a leading twentieth century British psychoanalyst, who first described these ideas as 'containment' (Bion, 1984). Containment might be described as offering or experiencing a safe 'breathing space'.

However, for many children and young people, particularly those on the autism spectrum, being able to express and find a language for feelings doesn't come easily. This means that it can be difficult for a significant other person (such as a parent or teacher) to find the right kind of language to offer that 'containment'. For autistic children, things like sensory overload, managing day-today transitions (like going to school) or waiting one's turn in a game can all trigger uncontainable meltdowns. The overwhelming feelings are often expressed by wailing and hitting or are suppressed through emotional shutdown and withdrawal. It's the children's difficulty with managing frustration, anxiety and sensory overload that creates the obstacles which get in the way of developing friendships and satisfying relationships. Parents and teachers often feel as helpless as the children when such meltdowns and shutdowns occur.

It's said that therapy is about removing the obstacles to growth. What I see time and time again in my work with children on the autism spectrum is that so often it is *anxiety* which is driving their behaviour and creating the greatest obstacle towards making relationships with others. So I wanted to see if there could be a way of working with children that could help them to not only reduce this anxiety, but also offer them an experience of what it feels like to be a part of a group, to have that sense of togetherness with others, and to make meaningful relationships with other children - so they could laugh and play. I wanted the children to have an experience of what it feels like to fit in and enjoy being different, without having to try and be 'like everyone else'. I wanted to create opportunities for children to be able to enjoy, appreciate and celebrate their individuality, while discovering there are other children who are similar to them.

The Friendly Group

In 1999 I set up the Friendly Group, which I describe as a social and therapeutic group for children with social communication difficulties, and which continues right up to the present. Rather than focusing on their difficulties as deficits, I wanted to draw out from the children the competencies that they already had. I truly believe that all children have the capacity to learn, and that learning comes from what they are already interested in and feel good at and about.

The Friendly Group is not a social skills group. The children are not explicitly taught anything. The structure and framework of the sessions offer containment, not instruction. As I say later in the book,

We are working on understanding what is happening between the children and ourselves (the adults) on any particular day. Instead of simply attending to what is being said, or how the children are behaving, which in therapeutic language is called the 'content', we are focusing on 'process' - making sense of the 'here-and-now' feelings about and experiences of what is happening.   p.82

The key principle of the Friendly Group is that it is a place where children can feel safe. Within that principle of safety there are seven aspects;

- **Containment** - including the physical environment and the framework of the sessions
- **Fostering the growth of relatedness** - where the children and young people are learning through direct experience
- **Authority** - learning to trust authority (both of the adults, and within the children and young people themselves)
- **Supporting the whole family** - parents are a part of the process
- **Being non-judgemental and kind** - recognising everyone's value through positive, caring and empathic relationships
- **Offering encouragement and appropriate challenge**
- **The Friendly Group** is a microcosm of the outside world of family and school

In this book I tell the story of how the Friendly Group came into being and describe the framework of the sessions. I explain about group process and the leadership role. Since the groups started there have been over two hundred children and young people who have been members, many for several years. This book tells the stories of some of these children and their parents, but they are told for all parents and all children.

I have altered identifying features to preserve confidentiality, but the dialogues and events are all true.

Some of the children's language may not sound very childlike; it might come across as rather formal. This reflects the way some children and young people on the autism spectrum speak. However, in the accounts, the words in the text are the actual words that they used.

A word about kindness

Every child who joins the Friendly Group is told that *"The people here are kind."* Kindness requires the ability to have empathy and a willingness to sometimes give up something that you might want to have or to do, for the sake of someone else. It is the ability to think about the feelings of someone else and to act in a way that you think might make that other person feel happier or better. It requires the ability to be patient, because patience is a form of kindness. There is a notice on the wall in the group room that says, *'One of the kindest things you can do is to listen to someone'*.

At first children might simply co-operate in taking turns, because that's what is expected of them in the group. They might reluctantly get off the trampoline to let someone else have a go, because an adult is standing there and suggesting it. At the end of most sessions the children are invited to share with one another any acts of kindness they have noticed in the group. To begin with many don't really understand what kindness is. They might repeat what another child has said, such as, *"She was friendly today,"* but cannot elaborate. However, as the children develop and the groups become established, connections are made between the children. A group history emerges, and a sense of belonging develops. True acts of kindness appear when the children begin to help one another.

Kindness is more than an altruistic act. It is about caring at an emotional level. When you realise you have helped someone, it increases sensitivity, confidence and self-awareness. Also, when you feel cared about and valued and you are able to reciprocate those gifts, meaningful relationships begin to develop. Friendship is about getting pleasure in putting someone else's desires before your own, and discovering that the other person is doing the same for you.

Finally

It has only been during the last twenty years that Autism Spectrum Disorder has entered the mainstream arena and begun to be better understood by the public in general. Before that it was a hidden and misunderstood disability within the fields of education and mental health. I've been an educational psychologist working with children since 1981 and have been on my own professional journey of learning and understanding what autism might be, which I share in Chapter 2, and I outline the importance of engaging the whole family in any support that is offered to a child on the autism spectrum in Chapter 3. In Chapters 4 and 5 I describe the framework, structure and resources used in the Friendly Group, which can be copied or adapted, if you are someone looking to set up your own group, or are a parent hoping to find a professional willing to do so. I discuss *how* groups work from a group analytical model in Chapters 6 and 7, and include thoughts about the leadership role (which could be both a leader of a group or a parent in a family group).

I wanted to write a book that told some of the children's stories, bringing to life the potency of group process. So the main part of the book is made up of these stories, which reflect common themes and struggles in the children and young people's lives: issues such as bullying, transitions, anxiety, trying to make friends, losses, meltdowns and illness.

However, this book is not just about children: it is about their parents too. You may be a parent reading this book and you may identify with other parents' experiences and challenges, or you may be a professional feeling you want to understand better what parents go through. I devote the whole of Chapter 15 to parents. I tell true stories of the common struggles that parents have and how important it is to find a support network. I hope that this chapter will also inspire professionals to set up more parents' support groups, as I am told repeatedly how many find them invaluable.

This book has taken me many years to write. There have been times when I nearly gave up. However, the parents of the Friendly Group children urged me to carry on because they wanted me to share with other people what is possible when children and young people on the autism spectrum work together as a group.

I hope that the stories you read here will give you hope, inspiration and insight such that, whether you are a parent, teacher or therapist, the children in your lives can also learn how to make friends too.

CHAPTER 1

It often starts like this

I am going to tell you a story about a nine year old boy (let's call him Colin), who, like all the children and young people who have been members of the Friendly Group, came to meet me before he joined.

It was very cold that day. The frost clung to the spiky grass near the door. When Colin arrived at the doorstep his cheeks were pink from the cold. On Colin's head was an old-fashioned man's cap. His coat was also old-fashioned, made of a tweedy material with large buttons down the front, which he had fastened right up to his neck.

"Come in!" I said, smiling in welcome, *"You must be Colin. It's cold out there so do come in to the warm and take your coat off." "I would prefer to keep my coat on, thank you,"* was the rather formal reply.

I led Colin through the hallway into a small room where we could sit down together. His mother, who had come with him, followed behind with a look of anxious concern on her face. I turned to give her a brief reassuring glance before paying attention to Colin. He walked into the room, looked around and remained standing.

"You can sit on the settee and make yourself comfortable," I said, gesturing towards a small blue sofa facing us. Colin's mother took off her coat and sat down. Colin remained standing with his hat and coat on. *"Come on Colin!*

Please take your coat off," said Colin's mother, in a tiny beseeching voice, almost whispering. *"I prefer to stay as I am,"* replied Colin clearly.

It didn't matter to me that Colin was standing in his protective armour. I understood the terror behind his formal language and his monotone voice. I had seen it before. And I had seen the anxious and helpless looks on his mother's face, in many other parents, anticipating possible disapproval or judgement.

"I do understand," I said and sat down in a small easy chair opposite the standing Colin and sitting mother.
"Now, Colin," I continued, *"You and I didn't arrange this visit, did we? It was your mother and I. I wonder why you think you have come to see me. You tell me first, then I will tell you why I think you have come and we can see if it's the same."* Colin looked down then glanced at his mother.
"I don't know ... it's something about a group or something," he mumbled.
"Yes! That's right! You have come today so that I can tell you something about the Friendly Group. First of all, though, I would like to tell you a story."
"But I don't like stories," was Colin's quick reply, *"I only like facts because they are true. Stories aren't true."*

In order to be able to appreciate fantasy, children need to feel something whole and secure inside them. Many children like Colin struggle to see the world in an integrated way. The world can often be confusing and fragmented to them and they seek the security of what is predictable.

"I can understand that you like facts, Colin," I said reassuringly, *"but stories are often about real things. They can explain things that are true. Stories can be funny and exciting as well."*

Colin winced as I said these words and his body stiffened as he stood soldier-like before me. His mother, on the other hand, looked at me with an eager expression, ready to hear what I had to say. I allowed a pause, time for Colin to process all these words I had spoken.

"I don't like stories because you don't know what's going to happen. There might be monsters and nasty things might happen," said Colin with some urgency in his voice.

Colin began to walk around the room and saw a bookshelf lined with books. He headed towards it but he was not looking at the books, he was looking at the space beneath the books. From my experience I guessed he was looking for a safe place under which he could retreat. Colin knelt down, and then wriggled into the enclosed space. He lay in a curled up foetal position and pulled the peak of his cap over his face. I wondered if, like many children, he could sense the floor beneath him and the shelf above him pressing on his shoulders. Maybe this felt comforting? His back and the balls of his feet were supported by the wall. When I could see that he was settled and that his mother had begun to relax on the sofa, I continued.

"It can feel scary when you don't know what's going to happen in a story. A bit like it must have felt coming here today."

Colin looked at me with a fixed stare that was not going to let his emotions show. It was as if he were uncertain whether I was going to ask something of him. He had the readiness of an alert animal anticipating flight from danger.

> *"Sometimes it feels scary when we don't feel in control."*
> *"Yes! I like to feel in control. My mum says I've got OCD. That's the word you use when you get obsessive about things. Its real name is obsessive compulsive disorder. I am obsessive about doing things in a special order before I go to bed. It takes ages but I couldn't go to bed and go to sleep if I didn't do these things,"* said Colin as he emerged slightly from his self-made cave.
> *"But we can't be in control of everything, can we? That's the tricky thing; working out how to manage when things get difficult."*

Colin looked up with an expression oscillating between suspicion and curiosity.

> *"You see, life is like an adventure story. You start on your journey when you are born and as you grow up you have experiences along the way. Some things are good but some are difficult. These experiences become the stories you tell about yourself."*

Colin then pushed back his cap and it fell off. He ignored it and let it lie upended on the floor near him. I could see that he had become curious.

> *"Why would I want to tell anyone about my experiences?"* he asked, stretching out his body. So I continued.
> *"I know it might sound odd but when we tell people things about ourselves,*

we actually find we get to know ourselves better. And it helps us get to know other people better too."

"But I don't see how that can happen?"

"Well, when you tell people about things that have happened to you, you might remember how you felt at the time. And if other people have had similar experiences and felt the same way, you might find you have something in common."

"I can't see the point in that," said Colin in an agitated tone.

I wondered if Colin often got agitated like this. He seemed to be trying to shut down this conversation. It looked like he was becoming uncertain about where this was going, and he didn't like it.

"It can give you good feelings when you find other people feel like you and do the same things as you. Friends are people like this. I don't know if this has happened to you?"

At these words, Colin emerged from under the shelf and sat up. He seemed interested now in where the conversation was going. I then expanded on these ideas.

"But it doesn't mean you can control other people's actions. You can't make other people play the games you like or be interested in the things you are interested in."

"What can you control then?" asked Colin.

"Maybe control is the wrong word," I said, without answering Colin's question.

His mother had already told me that Colin found it difficult to play with other children as he always wanted the play to be on his terms. When other children would not keep to his rules he became angry and the games fizzled out or the children left him. He then avoided them altogether.

> *"I don't understand what you are talking about!"* exclaimed Colin in a rather too loud voice. He now moved over to the sofa and sat down beside his mother, who was listening and watching silently and with interest.
> *"Well there's a difference between feeling in control of what you do and trying to control what someone else does. But it can feel good when you can let go of a bit of control."*
> *"Now I really don't know what you are talking about and it's getting boring,"* muttered Colin, pulling on his mother's sleeve.

He had had enough of this weird talk and wanted it to stop. I think what was really happening was that he wanted all these funny feelings that were going on inside him to stop. There was a part of him that understood the gist of what I was saying; that deeply sensitive side. But there was another part that seemed to put up the barriers against trusting and thinking about the uncomfortable feelings he was having. I wondered if Colin had got used to shutting himself off from other people as a way of coping. But it also meant he was isolated. He made himself different by wearing old-fashioned clothes, talking in a formal manner, avoiding playing or talking with other children of his age. It was as if he had modelled himself on an earlier, more formal and ordered era, and this kept others away. Even the way he buttoned his coat up to his neck looked like he was buttoning up his feelings.

Colin's mother had told me that he said he felt better if he kept away from others at school, but she could see that this separation only increased his anxiety and made him look different. In school, children have to sit near each other in the classroom and they get very close and noisy in changing rooms, the gym or when they have lunch in the dining room. The teachers tried to be kind. They let Colin eat lunch in a separate place and sit at a table by himself in the classroom, but this only confirmed he was different. He had never got to know how much in common he had with other boys.

> *"I wonder how it feels to come and see me today,"* I said with an encouraging smile, looking slightly away, so that my eyes did not feel like drills boring holes through his eyes. I let the words sink in.
> *"I don't know,"* replied Colin.
> *"I can understand that you might be feeling uncertain."*

I pointed to a small table on which were a bowl of biscuits, a jug of blackcurrant squash, a jug of water and three glasses, one for each of us in the room. Inviting Colin to help himself, I settled back in the chair for a few moments. Colin was looking puzzled now and I could see he was trying to make sense of our conversation. He was used to his mother taking him to see 'people who would help him get better', where the grown-ups talked about his problems in front of him as if he wasn't even there. He had now come to a place where the grown-up had said nothing to his mother at all and was talking to him about stories and control. What was this all about?

After initially refusing the offer, Colin went over to the table: the chocolate biscuits proving too alluring. I suggested to Colin that he could offer a biscuit to his mother, which he did by literally picking one from the bowl and taking it to her in one hand and with the other stuffing his own biscuit in his mouth, a trail of chocolatey crumbs tumbling onto the light blue carpet.

> *"Colin, that's not how you should behave in someone else's place. You're making a horrible mess. I've told you about this before,"* said his mother. These were the first words she had uttered. They betrayed her anxiety that I might judge her parenting or her son's clumsy social habits.
>
> *"That's alright! There has been much worse than a few crumbs on that carpet over the years!"* I said to reassure both of them. I turned to Colin. *"Colin! It could be a good idea to offer your mother the whole bowl of biscuits and then she can choose which one she wants to eat."*

Colin then returned to the table, replacing the biscuit, which had not yet reached his mother and returned offering the whole bowl. His mother took one and thanked Colin and he then offered me a biscuit.

> *"That's very kind of you,"* I said, *"but I don't want one at the moment. I can see you like these biscuits, though, so please have another one."*

Colin smiled for the very first time. His face lit up. I wondered if it was not just about having another biscuit, but also because he was beginning to see that I trusted and accepted him for who he was. I was not telling him off or putting him down. Indeed I was letting both Colin and his mother know that I liked them. I accepted them both.

> *"You have come to see me today, Colin, so that I can tell you about the Friendly Group. I hope you are going to try out the group on Saturday."*

I stopped to let Colin process this. I was unsure what Colin's mother had said to him about the purpose of this get together. Colin swallowed his biscuit in a gulp. I then carried on talking.

"It can be worrying when you start something new and don't know what's going to happen."

I paused to allow Colin to hear this. His brief eye contact communicated his agreement. I avoided asking all those awkward questions adults usually ask which can feel so intrusive and confusing. I continued by explaining that the group took place in the very room where we were that day. I explained how the furniture was moved out of the room, and how we all sat on cushions in a circle. I explained there were eight children of around his age and three grown-ups. I described the other two grown-ups, saying that none of us ever shouted. I explained that the group took place on a Saturday morning and lasted for one hour. Finally I went through the framework of the sessions, bringing out some of the resources like the stone and the *Bear Cards* (*see* Chapter 4) so Colin could actually feel and try these things out.

Colin listened to what I was saying, and slowly but surely he seemed to relax a bit: perhaps because he experienced no pressure from me. I was telling him things that were clear and factual. He had time to think and hopefully was beginning to trust me. He unbuttoned his coat and lent against his mother, stroking her leg. I answered his questions. I answered his mother's questions. I said that I hoped he would give the group a try and he said he would, but for one week only. That request isn't unusual. He would need to try it out to be sure.

THINGS TO THINK ABOUT

I wonder if you can identify with this story. Maybe you are a parent of a child who behaves like Colin? Maybe you are someone who works with children and who tries to put them at their ease when you first meet them?

As you probably know, when children are anxious and struggle to cope with social demands and expectations (as children and young people on the autism spectrum do), their behaviours can come across as rude, un-cooperative and even strange. However, what we all need to appreciate is that they will be doing their best to deal with their overwhelming feelings. It's therefore our responsibility as adults, whether parents or professionals, to try and make sense of what children's behaviours are telling us and acknowledge this. Even if we get it wrong, it is our *attempt to understand* which makes all the difference.

In the next chapter I'll share my understanding of the terms Asperger's Syndrome and Autism Spectrum Disorder and the way these two conditions overlap with attachment disorders. I'll also share my views on the benefits and drawbacks of diagnosis and how a child's difficulties are always related to those around them.

Autism Spectrum Disorder, Asperger's Syndrome and Attachment

How the Friendly Group came into being

It was because of an autistic boy called Morris and his mother, Amanda, that the Friendly Group started when and how it did. I had been working for many years in schools as a local authority Educational Psychologist and enjoyed my contact with parents and children. The focus of my work at that time (late 1980s to 1990s) was consultancy with school staff, and assessment of children's learning.

By the late 1990s, I felt I needed to make some changes to my career and decided to set up my own independent practice. I wanted to focus on therapeutic work with families. Before leaving I wrote letters to a number of parents with whom I'd worked for several years. One of the parents, Morris's mother Amanda, got in touch with me. She expressed regret that I was leaving the education services because she felt that her son had benefitted from the social group I was running at his school. She asked if I would consider running a group privately. It turned out that Amanda was the secretary of the local branch of the National Autistic Society and had many contacts. I said that if she could find three or four other children to join Morris then I would be happy to start a group. Amanda suggested that I write something about my plans for the group in the NAS newsletter, a four page paper edition posted out to the membership each month. These were the days before internet and websites! In September 1999, in collaboration with my colleague, Tess Miller, the Friendly Group was inaugurated with five children.

Autism Spectrum Disorder

In the late 1980s professionals and families knew little about Autism Spectrum Disorder (ASD) and I hardly met any children or young people with a diagnosis. Much of my knowledge up to that time was based on published biographical accounts by parents of children with severe autism; those who were unresponsive with respect to human relationships, had perplexing repetitive behaviours, no spoken language and were 'lost' in their own worlds.

It was the Austrian psychiatrist Leo Kanner, who first identified Autism Spectrum Disorder in 1943, following a study of eleven young children who presented with a combination of three features, which he described as:

- An extreme aloneness from the beginning of life
- An inability to use language meaningfully
- An anxiously obsessive insistence on the preservation of sameness

Initially he called the condition 'childhood psychosis' but later named it as autism. As his criteria for the diagnosis were very narrow, only a very few children were diagnosed. Autism was therefore seen as a very rare, debilitating and lifelong condition. Right from those early days there was academic debate as to whether autism had a biological cause or whether it was a result of the way in which children had been nurtured when they were babies.

To begin with, the nurturing theory became the more popular one. Families struggled when the mothers of these children were described by professionals as 'refrigerator mothers'. They felt isolated and blamed. The normal bonding with physical affection and maternal attunement to a baby's emotional needs was disrupted by these unresponsive babies. It therefore became doubly devastating to have a child with a diagnosis of autism. The rarity of the condition together with the uncertainty about its cause and the fact the children 'looked normal' gave it a mysterious and rather frightening quality to many people.

Following the multi-Oscar-winning film *Rain Man* starring Dustin Hoffman in 1988 (United Artists) public interest in and awareness of autism grew. However, unintentionally the film also created a perception that autistic people were generally like the Dustin Hoffman character who, as well as having very poor social communication skills, had special talents. In fact people with unusual talents (autistic savants as they are known) are very few and far between.

I have only met one or two children like this. In 1992 I remember visiting a family of a young boy who was severely autistic and had not yet started any formal education. He gave no visible response to my presence and was sitting quietly on his own as his parents spoke to me. The boy never uttered a sound during my whole visit. As I was leaving, the father told me that his son could say what the time was, even though he could not read a clock face and had no apparent understanding of time. He asked the boy what the time was and the boy's response was immediate and accurate to the minute. They were the only words he uttered. The family moved out of the area soon afterwards so I didn't have any further involvement with them, but the encounter made an impression on me because it was so unusual. This little boy was like the children I'd read about, and I wondered how his mind worked. Meeting him brought home to me how difficult it was for the parents, and I was struck by the father's desire to share his son's talent. It was as if he had thrown me a lifeline of hope that his child was 'good at something'. This talent had touched his father. He wanted a point of contact, some connection with his son.

During that same period, I visited another family, who had a three year old boy called Morris. This is the child I referred to at the beginning of the chapter. Morris's older sister was a sociable girl who had recently started school and was doing well. Morris, however, was very different from his sister. His parents told me that he had been diagnosed with Asperger's Syndrome. This was the first child I had ever met with this diagnosis. During my visit he clung to his mother and flinched and whimpered if our voices became raised or if we laughed. Eventually he felt settled enough to play on the floor with a few bricks, but he made no eye contact with me. I made no attempt to play with him as this would have created too much distress for him.

Morris's parents reported that he was developing some language skills and could communicate with his family, but was extremely anxious and shy of anyone outside the family. He became quickly distressed by unpredictable noises and movements and hated any changes to his rigid routines. My professional role was to assess Morris's special needs in order to make sure there was the right kind of preparation and support for him when he made the transition to school the following year. This was the start of a long relationship with Morris and his family, and my first direct and professional experience of children with Asperger's Syndrome.

Asperger's Syndrome

The syndrome got its name after the Austrian paediatrician Hans Asperger who was working with adolescent boys in the 1940s. At that time he was preparing his doctoral thesis and made a study of a group of boys who had difficulties integrating socially. He noticed certain unusual behavioural features common to this group and wrote about them. His doctoral thesis was published in 1944. The behavioural features Asperger identified were:

- Lack of empathy
- One-sided conversations
- Difficulties in forming friendships
- Pre-occupation in special interests
- Clumsy movements

However, it was the end of the Second World War, and there was little appetite at the time for material published in the German language. Hans Asperger's work was virtually unknown in the UK until the 1990s. It was Lorna Wing, an English psychiatrist, who came across Asperger's thesis and she was the first person to use the term Asperger's Syndrome in an academic paper she published in 1981. In 1989 Uta Frith, a German developmental psychologist (currently Emeritus Professor at University College, London), wrote a book called *Autism: Explaining the Enigma*, which broadened awareness about the syndrome, especially in academic and professional circles. Uta Frith also discovered Asperger's original paper when she was researching autism and managed to get it translated, fascinated with the links between the boys Asperger described as having 'autistic psychopathy' and those described by Leo Kanner.

It was a curious coincidence that Kanner (a psychiatrist) and Asperger (a paediatrician), who were both Austrian, were carrying out research on boys' impaired social behaviour and obsessive interests at virtually the same time. What is more, they both gave the same name of autism to describe the condition. However, the work of these two professionals was never shared. It was Kanner's definition of autism that became the prevalent model until recently. Diagnosis was based on Kanner's diagnostic criteria, consisting of a fairly narrow band of behaviours that included lack of responsiveness to other people and severe language impairment.

Uta Frith had been doing research on autism since the 1960s. The work of Asperger opened her eyes to the possibility of seeing autism as a much broader spectrum of ability and difficulty. She wrote fairly recently:

> Almost as soon as I had finished the *Enigma* book, I became hopelessly attracted to Asperger's Syndrome. With time I met an increasing number of unusual adults with a provisional diagnosis of autism, who amazed me because they were far

more able to converse than the now grown-up children whom I had first seen when I started doing research on autism in the 1960s. What struck me was their ability to provide insightful observations about their experiences. That opened up completely new possibilities to investigate the autistic mind. (Frith 2014 p.744)

Back in the 1990s, I began meeting more and more children diagnosed with Asperger's Syndrome. However the children were all so different, and their problems varied in so many ways, that it was difficult to gain a clear picture of what the diagnosis actually meant. Furthermore, in some clinicians' reports, the children had been given a double diagnosis, one of Asperger's Syndrome and the other, 'high functioning autism' implying a differentiation between the two. Other clinicians implied these two words meant the same thing. It all became rather confusing. Was autism the same as Asperger's Syndrome? If not, then what were the differences?

My professional colleagues (psychologists, psychiatrists and paediatricians) all had different views and perspectives. Increasingly reports became rather vague with terms such as *'autistic traits'*, *'mild autism'* and *'Asperger type behaviours'* being used rather than offering any clear diagnosis at all. I also noticed that once the words *'autistic traits'* or *'behaviours like Asperger's Syndrome'* appeared on a professional report (even if the report was written by someone not clinically trained to diagnose the condition), the children seemed to unofficially acquire a diagnosis and were then generally labelled as being autistic or having Asperger's Syndrome. Not surprisingly, parents felt very lost and confused, especially as a diagnosis brings with it fears of lifelong social and learning disabilities and dependency.

Identifying the Autism Spectrum

Lorna Wing (1996) helped to clarify the confusion by introducing, for the first time, the idea that autism is not confined to a specific set of clearly defined behaviours but needs to be seen as a broad *spectrum* of behaviours and characteristics. This was after years of work following a major study in 1978 that she and Judith Gould had carried out with children in Camberwell, South London. The notion of a spectrum gives one an understanding that there is both a range and type of disorder of increasing and decreasing severity. Asperger's Syndrome became the common term for those at the high functioning end of the spectrum. What is more, the notion of a spectrum removes the very narrow view of autism as it used to be. Increasingly we are becoming aware that we all share some characteristics of the spectrum! In 1998 Tony Attwood published his book *Asperger's Syndrome*, which became the 'bible' for professionals and parents alike. He described the six main areas of difference or characteristics regularly referenced by professionals. Children rarely present with all the various aspects of these characteristics but diagnosis is largely based on their number and frequency. The following develop the six areas Attwood described:

1. UNUSUAL SPEECH AND LANGUAGE
    - pragmatic language: using formal pedantic language or 'going on and on' in a social context
    - semantic language: not recognising that there may be several meanings for words and expressions, so taking things literally
    - prosody: using unusual pitch, stress or rhythm in speech

2. SOCIAL BEHAVIOUR

- little desire to socialise and interact with peers of the same age
- lack of appreciation of social cues
- poor ability to read facial expressions
- behaviours such as twirling, flapping, screaming and so on

3. INTERESTS AND ROUTINES

- obsessive fascination with special interests such as dinosaurs, trains and fossils, which may include making collections. Obsessive play of computer games or repetitive viewing of television programmes/films or YouTube clips
- routines such as the 'way' in which a child plays with toys or applies his or her special interest or carries out other activities like eating
- rigid rituals around times of transition such as going to bed, getting up in the morning, going to school, starting to do homework and so on
- changes to routine are extremely stressful as the predictability and order that are created by routine and ritual are disrupted

4. PHYSICAL CO-ORDINATION

- ungainly physical movements, such as walking without the associated arm swing or moving with a shuffling gait
- difficulties with manual dexterity where both hands are needed such as when eating with a knife and fork, tying shoe laces and zipping up a coat
- poor balance and problems with throwing and catching balls
- lax joints and difficulties with handwriting
- tics and frequent blinking

5. SENSORY SENSITIVITIES
- sensitivity to sounds: startle reaction to unexpected noises, poor tolerance of high pitched electrical noise (such as hand dryers and garden equipment) and multiples noises such as those in schools and shopping centres
- sensitivity to touch: physical affection can feel painful or overwhelming, bumping into someone can feel like an assault, cleaning teeth, brushing hair or wearing certain fabrics can be intolerable
- sensitivity to taste and texture of food and to certain smells
- sensitivity to light and colour
- low response levels to pain and temperature

6. THINKING, LEARNING, MEMORY AND IMAGINATION
- egocentric way of thinking - poor 'Theory of Mind,' which is the ability to imagine what another person may be thinking
- lack of empathy
- rigid thinking - so it is difficult to adapt to changes or failure, as children may only have one approach to a problem. This makes it difficult to learn from mistakes or apply learning (especially social learning) from one context to another
- excellent long term memory for facts, incidents in early life, film scenarios and so on
- talents in mathematical and computer skills
- vivid imagination but this is often expressed in a solitary way - a child is often unwilling to share his ideas or creative play. Also pretend play may include becoming an object rather than simply people or animals
- experiencing vivid dreams which can be recalled in detail

Emotional sensitivity and anxiety

I would also like to add a further sensitivity common to every child I have met on the autism spectrum, that seems to permeate all the other characteristics. I would describe it as *emotional sensitivity*. It triggers high levels of anxiety and creates difficulties for children as they struggle to manage their worries and confusion and to regulate their emotions. Parents regularly lament that their children have meltdowns and can go from one to ten (calm to rage) in a matter of a few seconds. What is more, the triggers can often seem (from an outside point of view) trivial, and be unforeseen. In the Friendly Group, much of the focus of the sessions is to help the children to think and talk about their emotions *as they are happening*. This facilitates self-awareness and improved regulation of their emotionally volcanic states. It's interesting how often volcanoes feature in the stories that are created in the group! (*and see* Chapters 8 and 11).

This emotional sensitivity also means that the children are often gentle souls, who would never deliberately set out to harm others. Indeed they can be easily wounded by the insensitive actions and lack of understanding of others. They are often very kind and generous and it saddens many parents to see their children being unable to show these positive aspects of themselves outside the home, where they get locked into defensive behaviours as a way of coping with the sensory and social onslaughts of the outside world.

"I love flowers and the way the sunshine makes them shine," said a boy recently, revealing his sensitivity to natural beauty. I've also noticed that many children who appreciate natural beauty also respond sensitively to animals and other living creatures. One member of the group used to bring bird seed each week and carefully place it in a bird feeder. Another member, who was terrified of spiders, nevertheless wanted their removal without any harm being done to them.

Another aspect of emotional sensitivity is the heightened sensitivity to the 'emotional temperature' of a social situation. While the children may struggle with empathy they nevertheless pick up on the 'vibes' of others and react to them without recognising or realising that is what has happened, or knowing how to process their responses to them. I have seen this time and time again in the Friendly Group as well as observing it in classrooms and playgrounds and hearing parents' accounts of family life. The children can be particularly sensitive to name calling, teenage banter, laughter and jokes. There is not only the risk that they might misunderstand when something is harmless, but they can also miss out on sharing laughter and fun, by becoming withdrawn, aggressive and very distressed. The Friendly Group offers a space for them to be able to think about their emotional responses towards other children as they are happening during the sessions, thus helping them to manage this sensitivity with greater awareness and confidence in other social situations.

'Aspie'

The term Asperger's Syndrome has become so well known that the shortened name 'Aspie', to describe someone with the syndrome, has now founds its way into common parlance. Adolescents and young people who are happy with their diagnosis often promote the term 'Aspie' as a badge of honour and there are also thousands of self-presentations of 'Aspies' on YouTube. The novel written by Mark Haddon *The Curious Incident of the Dog in the Night-time* (2003) has been a major influence in shaping the general view of Asperger's Syndrome. The novel gives a vivid account of a period in a teenage boy's life, which clearly describes the experience of being on the autism spectrum even though the terms autism and Asperger's Syndrome are never mentioned. The struggles that the character Christopher experiences in making sense of a world which he finds confusing and overwhelming, highlight the misunderstandings experienced not only by him but also by the people around him.

Over the last ten years, many of the parents I have worked with have given this novel to friends and family to educate them in their own children's problems and ways of seeing the world. They have found the book offers a very realistic description of the autistic experience. When I first read the book, I didn't like it. I felt the character was 'two dimensional' and lacked the emotional sensitivity of the children I was meeting on a weekly basis in the Friendly Group. However, in 2015 I saw a theatre production of the book, which altered my view! Christopher's emotional sensitivity seemed much more apparent when portrayed on stage. I was also touched by the enthusiastic response from an audience largely made up of young people, many of whom could have been on the autism spectrum.

While the term Asperger's Syndrome has now become well known, those updating the diagnostic assessment rating scales, the authors of the DSM-IV (Diagnostic and Statistical Manual of Mental Disorders) decided that Asperger's Syndrome was a good descriptor, but didn't fall into a separate category from autism. It didn't have its own clear boundaries or anything that qualitatively distinguishes it from autism. Subsequently there was the decision to scrap the term Asperger's Syndrome in the new DSM-5 assessment scale, and broaden the categories to create a single term of Autism Spectrum Disorder. However, I think that the term, Asperger's Syndrome, will continue to be used for quite some time.

Autism Spectrum Disorder and pathology: understanding the condition

DIAGNOSIS

In my thirty five years of professional life I have regularly experienced ambivalent feelings about the diagnosis of disorders associated with the way children think and learn. I know at a rational level that it's helpful to give names to create meaning and help one make sense of something, not least perplexing behaviour. I know that it's the way we learn language and how to communicate. We give things names; we imbue them with meaning. In early child development, children quickly learn that a living furry thing that barks does not just have a name like *dog,* it also fits into the category, *animal.* Being able to categorise helps us to memorise what would be impossible amounts of information. The ability to categorise and sort information is part of what psychologists call problem-solving.

So it makes sense that in order to understand how children learn to think, communicate and use their bodies, we create developmental categories to describe this, such as *short term memory skills, receptive language development, gross motor skills* and so on. Then within each category there are small sub-divisions to examine learning in greater and greater detail.

The diagnosis of learning difficulties also falls into categories. Let's take learning to read as an example. Children struggling with literacy skills might be diagnosed with one or more of the following; *dyslexia, dyspraxia, ADD (Attention deficit disorder), ADHD (attention deficit hyperactive disorder), moderate learning difficulties, semantic pragmatic language disorder*, to name but a few. ASD (Autism Spectrum Disorder) can also affect children's ability to develop literacy skills, especially with interpretation of text and understanding inference, because so many ASD children have a rather functional, rigid and literal way of interpreting language.

AMBIVALENCE ABOUT DIAGNOSIS

So why do I often feel such ambivalence about diagnosis? Surely it can only help a child? Before I answer these questions I'd like to share some of the common feelings of the ambivalence felt by parents who suspect their child is on the autism spectrum, or whose child has already been given a diagnosis:

> I have just received a diagnosis for my daughter and I feel that I have been dropped in a big sea and I'm drowning

> I have just had my child diagnosed with ASD but I don't I know whether I should tell him or not

> I don't know what to do. I think my child may be autistic but I don't feel ready for a diagnosis

> I have told my child she has Asperger's Syndrome and it has made her really unhappy. She feels there is something wrong with her and now she just wants to get better. We don't know what to say

> I'm no longer Sam's mother; I am the mother of the autistic boy and although some people are kind it feels more like pity than friendliness

> I want to get a diagnosis for my son but my husband is against it. He says there is nothing wrong with our son. I think my husband is on the spectrum

> Since the diagnosis, my child's behaviour has got worse and worse. Whenever I tell him off or ask him to do anything he doesn't want to he's just defiant and rude and refuses me, saying he can't because he's got Asperger's. He tells me I don't understand him and shouldn't stress him

Long before the diagnosis of Asperger's Syndrome and ASD became so prevalent, I regularly met parents whose children had been diagnosed with other conditions such as *dyslexia, dyspraxia* and *ADHD*. While a diagnosis can undoubtedly be helpful, I also discovered some worrying and prevalent outcomes and consequences. It often created a 'can't do' mentality from all concerned. Parents, teachers and children alike could sometimes 'hide' behind the diagnosis when things are not going as well as everyone wanted: *"Oh she's like that because she got dyslexia," "He can never concentrate on written work because of his ADHD," "I couldn't finish my homework because of my dyspraxia."*

What was worrying to me was the potentially limiting nature of a diagnosis, the sense of everyone lowering their expectations about what a child might be able to learn and to achieve. It concerned me that the children and young people who were either rather passive in nature or who struggled emotionally in the face of challenge and gave up easily, also quickly developed secondary problems of poor resilience. These secondary problems were learnt behaviours that the children used in order to avoid trying something new or to give up in the face of difficulty. These behaviours could range from being disruptive and attention-seeking in the classroom, to being highly dependent on someone else to help get them started on a task or to follow instructions or whatever. The secondary problems often became much more of a block to learning than the initial diagnosed learning difficulty. This continues to be a big problem today.

Another of my concerns has been the rising use of pharmaceutical medications for children, particularly for children who have been diagnosed with ADHD. While careful use has been of benefit to many children, I have seen far more who have had physiological problems (such as poor appetite, numbness and disruptive sleep) and psychological problems (such as feeling a bad person unless they take their medication) to alert me that we need to be very careful when treating and helping children.

BEWARE OF PATHOLOGISING

So what about my feelings towards the diagnosis of Asperger's Syndrome and Autism Spectrum Disorder? My views have developed and changed over the years as a result of the experiences I've had meeting and working with children and their families and through running the Friendly Group.

On meeting parents, I tell them that I want to get to know their children as *people* in their own right first and without a diagnostic tag to their name. The essence of that sentiment is still with me, because it can be easy to explain worrying behaviours through the lens of a disorder and ignore the normal interplay between the developing personality and environmental conditions. For example, all children respond well to routine and have times of intense interest in their play, not just those on the autism spectrum. There is a natural fluidity in the development of childhood and adolescence. I like the view of the neurologist Oliver Sachs, who said he looked for the person in the disorder rather than the disorder in the person. I am always searching for ways to get to know the personality and spirit behind the figure who might be jumping, flapping, flicking, displaying tics, hiding, interrupting or going on and on about a latest obsessive interest in an unusual tone of voice.

The trouble with terms like 'disorder' and 'syndrome' is that they conjure up pathology, a sense of something being wrong that needs to be put right or cured. In her research (2003), Uta Frith placed her emphasis on *qualitative differences* in the way a child thinks or responds, and searched for the benefits of those differences. I know that I've probably erred on that more positive outlook in the way I approach my work with parents and children. I look for a child's individuality and personal qualities and the differences that make them interesting as people. I look for their strengths and I want to know about their interests, what makes them laugh or how they are soothed and comforted. However, searching for strengths can itself can have limitations because, caught up in the enthusiasm of looking for the positives, one can inadvertently miss the genuine difficulties that a child, who does think differently, might be facing. Indeed, while all children need comfort to alleviate sources of stress, there is a difference between the child who seeks a parental cuddle or a teddy comforter and the child who is soothed by gazing at the rotating drum in a washing machine or by lining up his toy dinosaurs.

So, diagnosis can have its benefits. The following extract from a recent email that I received from a parent echoes the sentiments of many parents for whom the diagnosis has been both a relief and a pathway towards better understanding.

> While we both felt profoundly sad to have the diagnosis, an equal emotion was relief. Now we knew what it was about Solomon that made him seem different. Now we knew that it wasn't our parenting that was at fault. Now we understood why he would refuse to get in the car to go on holiday, or get so upset about getting on a train to go on a day trip to London.
>
> It was quite a breakthrough moment to realise that Solomon's difficult behaviour was born of anxiety rather than sheer waywardness.
>
> The diagnosis was also empowering as it meant we could take action; we had a syndrome we could research and discuss. We could now attend courses and get other professional help. In another sense, though, the diagnosis was also crushing, but in the end we have found that having a name for Solomon's difficulties is much better that not knowing what was wrong.

Underlying anxiety

What I say to parents of children attending the Friendly Group is that whatever the actual diagnosis, the underlying feature connecting all of them is the *high levels of anxiety* they experience, which arise from either emotional or sensory sensitivity, or both. The affirming parental nods and grunts inform me that they agree about this anxiety issue which not only drives their children but also holds them back. Anxiety often manifests when a child feels overwhelmed and they have no power to deal with something they are frightened of. Autistic children fear novelty and change and so they try and reduce their anxiety by 'taking control' through their rigid behaviours, routines and repetitive play. Anxiety drives them to stick to the things that are familiar (including eating the same foods and wearing the same clothes) and makes it very difficult for them to try new things, go to new places and meet new people. Novelty is exciting for most children. It is what normally developing children seek out to stimulate their thirst for learning and meaning. For children on the autism spectrum novelty is at best daunting, and at worst, completely overwhelming. Anxiety completely takes over and can paralyse children's natural curiosity.

But there can be many reasons for a child's behaviours that suggest high levels of anxiety. This has contributed to my reserve over the specific label of autism as a blanket explanation for a child's presenting difficulties. Childhood traumas like premature birth, surgical procedures, accidents, violence, neglect, emotional abuse, death or unexpected separation of a parent or caregiver all trigger anxiety in babies and children. Anxiety disorders in mothers, such as post-natal depression, can also affect development, particularly at the early stage of attachment, that early infant bonding with a mother. Professionals need to work together to support families as a whole and beware of simply focusing on the child as the sole source of any problem.

Attachment Theory

Alongside Asperger's Syndrome becoming better known in recent years, so has our understanding of early infant development and attachment behaviours. *Attachment* is the term used to describe the way babies bond with their parents and caregivers and how this affects the way they develop emotional regulation and resilience, empathy and social relationships. It was John Bowlby (1969) and Donald Winnicott (1964) who worked extensively with children and their families and wrote, in the mid-twentieth century, about the importance of early infant bonding with their mothers and the need for mothers to be attuned and responsive to their babies. They showed how this is necessary for babies and young children to be able to develop emotional security as well as the ability to play, learn and relate to others.

Bowlby developed what is known as *Attachment Theory* and described different types of attachment, both secure and insecure. Attachment theory went out of fashion during the late twentieth century, and has only returned in the last decade when its essential relevance and importance was once again appreciated. I was never taught about it during my academic training in the late 1970s and early 1980s. Maybe this was a reaction against the simplistic interpretation that parents could be 'blamed' for a child's emotional insecurity. However, technological advances in the last 15 years have created the opportunity for a greater understanding of early child development through the use of sophisticated brain scanning techniques. Scientists like Alan Schore (2001, 2003) have been able to examine baby's and children's brains and discover even more about the sensitivity of a baby's brain to the affection and responsiveness he or she receives. I remember, around the year 2000, the enthusiasm with which Alan Schore shared his research at a conference I attended. There was no sense of blame, rather a greater sensitivity towards the impact of the stresses facing parents in our current culture and how this affects our babies and children.

Advances in biochemistry too have enabled scientists to understand the corrosive impact of excessive cortisol, one of the hormones that flood a baby or child's nervous system if they are under stress, for example feeling anxious or insecure. It is a part of normal development to learn how to manage stress, and the interaction of brain activity and natural levels of cortisol play their part in this. However, research has also shown that high cortisol levels are linked to high activity in the parts of the brain which generate fearfulness, irritability and withdrawal from others. High levels of cortisol can equally interfere with the normal development of other parts of the brain related to emotional regulation, and cognitive reasoning based on this. Modern technology and biochemistry are now confirming the validity and the importance of Bowlby's and Winnicott's theoretical models. Sue Gerhardt's book *Why Love Matters* (2004) brought much of this research together for the first time, generating yet further research and discussion among professionals. There continue to be important discoveries and further understanding in this important field.

The overlap between Autism Spectrum Disorder and attachment disorders

It was with this backdrop that in the early days of the Friendly Group I found myself wondering to what extent the children's anxiety and associated social difficulties were linked to attachment difficulties rather than as a result of Autism Spectrum Disorder. I have since come to realise that it is not an 'either/or' scenario. There is always overlap. The very nature of autism, where children often have difficulty with eye contact (the very first bonding behaviour) and are not easily soothed with cuddles and cooing, due to heightened sensory sensitivity, makes it difficult for both parents and their babies to bond in the normal way anyway. For children on the autism spectrum, there is almost always some kind of disruption in the bonding process. It is nobody's fault. It is unimaginably difficult as a parent of a baby who does not sleep, or who is unresponsive, or who does not stop screaming, (whatever the reasons) to be emotionally available, attuned and relaxed.

The difficulties of identifying whether or not a child with attachment problems also has Autism Spectrum Disorder are being examined by clinicians throughout the country. At a conference I attended in 2012 (organised by the British Psychological Society) Heather Moran presented the Coventry Grid which maps out features of autism spectrum and attachment disorders and common problems of both conditions and typical behaviours in each. She described that when the research group was creating the grid, there was lively debate about what constituted similarities and differences. In essence, it was agreed that the autistic child tends to approach the world from a cognitive frame of reference (thinking and reasoning) and tries to make the world fit with his preferences: whereas the child with attachment disorders approaches the world from a relational and emotional frame of reference. For example rigid, obsessive behaviours and tantrums, associated with eating, arose in both groups. The differences lay in how, when and where they occurred. The children on the autism spectrum struggled with the taste and texture of food. The children with attachment problems had difficulties which were much more related to their emotional response to food and particularly over who was offering it or how much they'd get.

It was interesting to also read in Moran's paper (2010 p, 46) that:

> Professionals described a much more 'emotional feel' to therapeutic relationships with children with attachment problems and a more 'matter-of-fact' feel to therapeutic relationships with those on the autism spectrum.

I would agree with that general observation. When children join the Friendly Group they often show more interest in the session framework and the physical environment than on finding out about the other children. It is for these reasons that we pay particular attention to the 'dynamic administration' of the sessions, such as making sure the cushions are laid out ready in a circle, the toys are in the same place and we follow the same structure. When the children begin to feel safe within reliable boundaries of physical sameness, they begin to show more interest in the other children and developing relationships follow.

Relationship becomes more important than diagnosis and targets

Part of any professional practice in the field of therapeutic work involves supervision. This is giving time for reflection about the clients, outside of sessions with a qualified colleague. Reflective work also includes journal and note writing. Below is an extract from my journal in September 2015.

Therapy is not about targets. It's about relationships. I see the autistic child who is withdrawn and uncurious (locked in, really) and does not join in the group but then is drawn out, drawn into the group by other children's empathy, understanding and benign tolerance and patience.

When they become drawn in by other children who are like themselves, it creates a little bit of connection - like a little 'thread'. That 'thread' is what pulls the child out of the 'locked in' place, and they begin to get a sense of another person (a child or adult), rather than just themselves. They begin to experience a little bit of 'belonging' in the group. And as, week after week, small links between children are made, more and more threads are woven into the fabric of shared experience and meaning. They begin to know what it feels like to be part of something. As the children begin to help each they get past the narcissistic state of 'all about me' and move into 'you and me'.

Then there is the question of what we mean when we tell parents their child is making progress. What do we mean by progress? We don't give clear targets or goals for change which can be measured. No! We simply share moments when we have seen a little shift in their child's behaviour towards joining in, playing, laughing, sharing, talking about their feelings or relaxing. Or when their child has demonstrated an act of kindness or been able to talk about their fears.

I know the parents trust us, but why? And what do they trust? I wonder to what extent we become secure attachment figures for them and their children. Initially, they might feel they can trust us because we have many years of professional experience and a good local reputation. However in the long term what matters are the relationships we create together.

The difficulties are not just a child's own

Children with any difficulties, whether these have a diagnostic label or not, are vulnerable at two levels. At one level their difficulties can make it more of a challenge to learn, fit in, or feel emotionally at ease. At another level they become reliant on the adults around them, their parents, carers, teachers and other professionals, to help them. Sadly, not all children or young people have reliable care from adults. What is more, a child's difficulties are never just their own. Children live in families and spend time in nurseries and schools. Their difficulties impinge on the adults, siblings and peers and vice versa. It's easy to focus on a particular member of the family or class group as the 'problem'. However, a child's problems are always related to those around them. When a child or young person on the autism spectrum screams because cleaning teeth or putting socks on is painful, for example, this is not only a problem to that child but also to the parent who is trying to get the child ready in time for school. What about the other children in the family if they have any siblings?

It can be a burden to a sibling to have to learn to accommodate the anxieties and intolerances of a brother or sister, when they themselves might be feeling anxious or want to complain or seek comfort. There was a case recently, when I was working with a family who had a thirteen year old daughter on the autism spectrum and a nine year old daughter who had no developmental difficulties. Initially, the parents sought my help because the mother found the demands from her autistic daughter overwhelming. The younger sister had learnt to take on the role of the 'good daughter' and to repress her emotions, but at times, like a pressure cooker, they intensified to the point where she would sometimes burst into unexpected angry outbursts. When the whole family worked together, the two sisters were able to share their feelings about each other on equal terms. They both benefitted, as the younger sister now felt included and the older sister did not bear the burden of being the 'named one' with the problems. The whole family then began to find different ways to communicate their feelings with each other and to understand each other better.

> **THINGS TO THINK ABOUT**
>
> As a parent it can be difficult to know whether or not to seek a diagnosis for your child, if you suspect autism. Maybe this is the case for you? If you already have a diagnosis, then the timing of telling your child becomes another worry and challenge. Those of us in a professional role can easily underestimate these parental dilemmas and worries; a diagnosis can be both a relief and a terrifying prospect. Autism appears to be for life, and it's this that can be very frightening for families.
>
> However, it must be remembered that autism is also a developmental condition, so autistic children do mature and develop as all children do. What's more, as the assessment process involves subjective judgement through the completion of questionnaires, the prognosis is also subjective. Children can be very surprising, especially if we have faith in what they can do.
>
> I feel it's more helpful to view autism as a different way of seeing the world. Many children I meet tell me that, *"I have autism and that means my brain works differently from most people."* The autism label gives them an explanation as to why they sometimes don't 'get' other people or other people don't 'get' them. If children are given the opportunity to actively learn how to manage their emotions, develop empathy and socialise with more ease within a sympathetic and understanding peer group, then their learning will accelerate and they will feel good about themselves.
>
> *"When should I tell my child?"* is a question often asked by parents. I have a simple

answer to this. *"Wait until they begin to ask you why they are different or why they get so worried or find it so difficult to make friends."* These are clues that tell us they are ready. If a child is still innocently unaware of their differences or is in deep denial, then it could feel too overwhelming to try to process the information.

In the next chapter we'll look at how we help to prepare not only the child, but their parents too before joining the Friendly Group. Given the sensitivities and anxieties of all children on the autism spectrum, which I outlined in this chapter, you will see how important it is to take care in addressing parental and child concerns and questions. The better the preparation (for everyone) the more successful any therapeutic intervention is likely to be. What follows is based directly on my own professional experience, although the identities of those in the stories have naturally been slightly changed to preserve anonymity.

Preparation for the Friendly Group - a family commitment

The Friendly Group is for the entire family

When parents first get in contact with us to make enquiries about their child attending the Friendly Group, we always suggest an initial meeting so we can begin to get to know one another. How can a parent feel confident about entrusting their child to the group unless we have begun to establish some trust between us first? Before the meeting we will have sent information about the group including aims, timings, fees and how payments are made, so that parents will have already had some of the more practical information.

This first meeting not only allows us to explain what happens in the group but also provides an opportunity to gain some understanding of the family dynamic. It's easy to simply focus on the child's difficulties: but any disturbance and struggles will always be felt within the family as a whole, and not just within the child. The children and young people who get the most out of the Friendly Group are those whose parents are actively interested and involved. This doesn't mean that parents attend the group, they're not present during sessions. In fact there is a clear physical boundary between the children and young people's space and the publicly shared space where they can drop off their children or wait to pick them up.

The importance of involving parents

What I mean by parental involvement is:

- A willingness to meet with a group leader before their child starts the group
- An interest in understanding how the group works
- A trust that their child's confidence and social competence will emerge in their own time
- Participating in the informal parent group (*more detail in* Chapter 15 *The Café Group*)
- Attending the parents' evening session once each term
- Arriving promptly for the start of the session and picking up their children punctually at the end
- A willingness to ask questions or have individual sessions, when there are concerns or when a parent wants advice
- Respecting the physical boundaries of the environment, so their child knows when and where we, the leaders, are in charge and when and where they, the parents, are in charge

I would say, however, that the most important way a parent can support the work in the group is to demonstrate to their child their own confidence in it. This is because the Friendly Group will feel a safe place, to even the most anxious child, if their parents feel that it is.

Questions commonly asked by parents

Parents are naturally interested and concerned regarding what happens in the Friendly Group, how it works and who the other children are. Here are some of the commonly asked questions that come up when we first meet parents. If you want to run a similar group then you might find these questions useful for your own planning and thinking. If you are a parent looking for a group, or if your child is about to start a group, then you might want to ask some of these questions yourself.

Q1 DO ALL THE CHILDREN IN THE GROUP HAVE A DIAGNOSIS?

While many of the children do have a diagnosis of Asperger's Syndrome or Autism Spectrum Disorder, this is not always the case. Some children have been diagnosed with other conditions such as ADHD (when children cannot sit still or concentrate easily), dyspraxia (when children have co-ordination and organisational problems), semantic pragmatic language disorder (when children take language literally) and other language and learning difficulties. Some children have no diagnosis at all.

Q2 HOW ARE CHILDREN REFERRED TO THE GROUP?

There is no formal referral system as such because of the independent status of the Friendly Group. The group is recommended to some parents by their GP, paediatrician or school SENCO (special needs co-ordinator). The group is also recommended to other parents by educational psychologists, speech and language therapists or occupational therapists, (those who have carried out assessments on their child). Many parents contact us on the recommendation of other parents either personally or through social networking on the internet.

Q3 I HAVE NOT TOLD MY CHILD THAT HE HAS ASPERGER'S SYNDROME AND I AM WORRIED THAT YOU MIGHT DISCUSS THIS IN THE GROUP. DO YOU BRING THIS UP?

The subject of Autism Spectrum Disorder or Asperger's Syndrome does come up from time to time in the group. It is usually raised by one of the children, who asks if anyone else 'has it' or what 'it is'. Occasionally we introduce it quite naturally, when it feels appropriate and therapeutically beneficial such as when the children want to talk about feeling left out and being different. When children recognise that many of them share a condition and that it is safe and acceptable to talk about it, this can be very liberating and supportive for them. However, if a parent has specifically asked us not to mention the subject then we will respect that request until the family is ready.

Q4 MY CHILD HAS RECENTLY HAD A DIAGNOSIS OF ASD (AUTISM SPECTRUM DISORDER) AND WOULD LIKE TO TALK ABOUT IT IN THE GROUP. IS THIS ALRIGHT?

It is alright for a child to bring anything up that they want to share in the group. My colleagues and I will guide and support this for the benefit of everyone in the group. We are sensitive towards all the children and how they might be feeling about any subject that comes up or any behaviour that is acted out.

Q5 DO YOU GIVE ANY FEEDBACK ABOUT WHAT THE CHILDREN TELL YOU IN THE GROUP?

That is a very important question and the answer is "Yes we do" and the children are aware that my colleagues and I talk to their parents. There is also an evening session once a term for parents where we agree to talk openly with each other. However, we need to use our judgement about how much we share. Anyone doing this kind of therapeutic work needs to give this matter a lot of careful consideration. In the group we explain to the children that what we talk about is not a matter for gossip. Other people's 'stuff' is not theirs to share; learning about these kinds of boundaries is a useful and important social skill for them. The children also need to feel that it is safe to talk about personal issues and feelings in a private way.

When children want to be private, then that is respected. Some things can be private and we all know how important that is, but it is not the same as being secret, which is unhealthy. Being private is about being able to discern with whom we can share our 'insides' and recognising that we don't have to answer personal questions. I have noticed that when children reach the age of about eleven or twelve, some of them begin to become concerned about what we might tell their parents. Some don't want to burden their parents with their worries, and others feel embarrassed about their personal issues, like all young people who reach puberty and become more self conscious. We try to take our guidance from the young people as far as possible.

Naturally we would act according to professional guidelines were a child to disclose something that was a child protection or safeguarding issue.

Q6 MY CHILD IS VERY ANXIOUS AND GETS AGITATED WITH OTHER CHILDREN. HOW DO YOU MANAGE THIS?

The way we help the children is to acknowledge that anxiety or agitation when it happens. We help the children to notice how they are feeling and hopefully say how they feel. When one child is agitated, it will be affecting the others too and by acknowledging this with the whole group, feelings of anxiety are greatly reduced. I will give you an example so you will have a better idea of how we do this.

DOUGLAS'S STORY

On arrival for his first session, Douglas (11) was initially very talkative. I was aware that this behaviour was one of the ways he covered up his anxiety. Another of his strategies was to say what he thought was the 'right thing' to please others.

During the session the children were invited to choose a Bear Card portraying their feelings about coming to the group (the Bear Cards are explained in Chapter 4). Douglas chose one with a bear that looked very worried and placed the card face down. As the others began to talk about the cards they had chosen, Douglas pulled the hood of his sweatshirt over his head. This wasn't enough. Soon his head dropped down. A moment later he pulled the hood right over his face and from a kneeling position, placed his head face down on the floor. His behaviour was a clear communication that he was finding the group's talk about their feelings too much for him.

When it was his turn, Douglas didn't want to show his card. My colleague Claire, who was sitting beside him, lent forward and offered to turn it over for him, saying in a quiet voice, *"Maybe you would like me to turn your card over to show the others?"* Douglas gave an affirmative nod from this face-down position but didn't raise his head. Claire continued by suggesting that the bear looked rather anxious and worried, and maybe that was how he felt? Once again, Douglas nodded from this face-down position.

At this, some of the children in the group said they knew exactly how Douglas felt. They had also felt worried when they started the group. A short time later, Douglas slowly sat up and pulled back his hood. He needed time for the experience of the group's empathic understanding to sink in. By the end of the session he began to smile a little and was able to tell the group about how he had felt anxious at first but he felt better now that he had met everyone.

Q7 I AM WORRIED THAT MY CHILD MIGHT SEE INAPPROPRIATE BEHAVIOUR IN THE GROUP AND MIGHT COPY IT. WHAT DO YOU DO ABOUT THIS?

We make sure that there are clear guidelines for the children about what is acceptable and unacceptable behaviour in the group. This gives them structure within which they can feel safe. However, unlike at school, there is greater flexibility here about acceptable behaviours, like lying on the floor (when a child needs to feel grounded), fiddling with an object (to help those who find sitting still difficult), sitting in the adjoining room (when a child is feeling emotionally overwhelmed), jumping and hand flapping (when aroused). Behaviour would only be considered inappropriate if it is distressing another person or making them feel uncomfortable, such as kicking, throwing, shouting or swearing. The adults intervene at that point.

However we recognise that behaviour is a powerful form of communication. Behavioural styles can also become habits. During the sessions, we invite the group to say how they feel about another child's behaviour. Invariably the group is understanding, tolerant and supportive, which helps all of them. For a child to hear that one of his peers doesn't mind, if, for example, he is in the other room, or is lying on the floor or is not speaking, is very comforting. Copying of inappropriate behaviour only happens when that behaviour remains unspoken about.

Q8 HOW LONG IS EACH SESSION AND HOW LONG DOES A CHILD STAY IN THE GROUP? AND WHAT ABOUT COSTS?

The session lasts for one hour but children can arrive up to ten minutes early so that they can settle in before we make a start in the circle together. There is a set of six sessions each term. Children can attend the group for up to four or five years or until the end of school Year 11, but their place is reviewed with them and their parents each year. Most children stay for about three years and leave when they feel they have the confidence to pursue other interests, and/or have got as much as they want to out of the group. The Friendly Group is privately run, so there is a fee. However, if you were to find a group run in a school, let's say, then the funding might be paid through the local authority. Local groups will undoubtedly find local solutions.

Initial hopes

There is no doubt that the Friendly Group is effective when there is noticeable progress, which the children recognise themselves. The parents usually see this progress even before the children do. However the knotty question of how much this is due to the particular therapeutic approaches or techniques, and how much is due to the quality of the relationships, is impossible to fully unravel. What is certain, and underlies all the work we do, is that we (the group leaders) cultivate genuine and empathic relationships with all of the children and share genuine hope and belief in their capacity for change, growth and development.

Usually parents hope that their child will be happy, confident and make friends. If you are a parent then you will probably agree with these hopes. Indeed, the fact that the children actually want to come to the group is a great relief to parents, and all parents comment on their child's increasing confidence.

The individual visit before starting the Friendly Group

When my colleagues or I meet a child for the first time, they will be brought by one or both of their parents. At the beginning of this session, the parents take on an observer role which I will have briefed them on in the earlier meeting. This is because I want to be free to devote my attention to the child or young person. I want to get to know him or her as an individual with personality, sensitivities, interests, fears, and so on. I also want the child to begin to get to know and trust me and the environment in which we'll both be working. As the session develops, I invite the parents to participate, allowing me some first-hand glimpses into the family dynamic and how the family's relationships, their behaviours and communication styles affect each other.

This session also allows me to assess the way a child communicates and how they deal with a new situation. I am mindfully aware of their underlying anxiety, whatever their outward behaviour. Indeed I pay particular attention to the energy and behaviour the child brings to the encounter so that I can respond in ways that I hope will feel comfortable for them. I show my natural interest in the child which not only helps them to feel more at ease, but is also reassuring to the parents. Another value of this visit is that it takes away some of the uncertainty for the child before the first group session. He or she knows what I look like and what my voice sounds like. They can see what the entrance is like and what the room and the garden look like. When describing my colleagues, (giving their names, where they usually sit in the room and so on) I offer to show photos of them too.

I explain how the room is set up, and I show and use the resources we have. I explain the framework of the session, using a picture poster, and invite questions as I go along. I also give the names of the other group members, say what time the group starts, how long it goes on for, and where he or she will enter and leave, including where the parents wait. The greater the detail, the more interested and less anxious the children become.

I am mindful of the fact that if you are a council employed professional you may feel you don't have the time for this kind of preparation. However, its value can easily be underestimated, so it's worth thinking about how you might prepare families in ways that could work for you, and for them.

Children do not choose to come to the Friendly Group

Unlike a group for adults, where members choose to attend, the Friendly Group children join because their parents have made that choice for them. The children are usually reluctant and often protest (at home beforehand) about coming. What helps the children to make a commitment is for them to feel and see that their parents get on with my colleagues and me and have confidence in the group. It's even better if the parents have some understanding of how the group works and appreciate the importance of the child's private visit just before their first group session.

It's easy to misunderstand the group at first as it is rather unusual, being a social and therapeutic group. Some parents imagine that it is a social club where, in a safe environment, their children will simply have the opportunity to play and socialise with others who have similar difficulties. Others see it as a social skills group and are hoping that we will teach specific skills to their children.

We explain that the Friendly Group is neither of these things. Rather, the group offers a place of support where the children can begin to talk about themselves and share their feelings with one another. They are accepted and appreciated by the adults for who they are, and this is the starting point for learning. The adults guide the children in being able to express their worries and the children then support each other. It is this peer understanding and support that facilitates connection and the beginnings of empathy between the children. However, I should also say that the children do also have fun and learn through their play!

Children's feelings on the first day

NEIL'S STORY

Neil (14) had managed to get by at school without too many obvious difficulties. He did his schoolwork, he did his homework and he hung around the fringe of his peer group. He caused no trouble. He was 'under the radar', as it were. None of the adults at school noticed how alone he was. But his parents began to get worried when Neil stayed at home while his brother (12) began meeting up in town with his friends, playing online computer games with them, playing football on the local recreational ground or going to each other's houses.

Neil simply came home straight from school and stayed at home every evening, every weekend and every holiday. He told his parents he had friends, but they had never met any since he started senior school. They encouraged him to make contact with some of them but his phone was unused.

Then his parents began to notice that what they had thought was simply teenage awkwardness seemed to be something more. He didn't 'get' jokes in the family; he became confused by some of the television programmes, only following the dialogue at a rather literal level. There seemed to be some rigid rituals developing in the daily routines of getting up and going to bed. Neil's parents took him for an assessment and he was diagnosed as having high functioning autism, after which it was suggested that he join the Friendly Group.

Although I had already met Neil before this first group session, he barely gave me a glance of recognition as he entered the room. He walked in with a kind of swagger, surveyed the other youngsters with expert discretion before finding a cushion on which to sit. Sporting the latest haircut and wearing fashionable clothes, he adopted what he probably felt was a 'cool' sitting pose, phone casually in his hand. Once he had got his place, he looked at the other youngsters with a sidelong glance as if he were studying what kind of people they were. Neil didn't believe that the group could be helpful. He had told his parents that he was OK; there was nothing wrong with him and he didn't want to go. He said he was worried that the group would be full of those people that at school were called 'nerds' or 'geeks'. He certainly didn't want to be classed among people like them. But Neil was also a boy who didn't make an outward fuss and went along with what his parents asked of him, so he had arrived on time that Saturday.

After welcoming him, Neil was quietly asked to turn off his phone and put it away and he quickly co-operated. Part-way through the session, the Bear Cards were spread out in the middle of the circle.

"Pick up a card of a bear that looks like you felt when starting the Friendly Group for the very first time," I said. After a pause I continued, to the whole group: *"Some of you might find it hard to remember, so maybe you could*

imagine it? Others of you might well remember as it is not very long ago, and if you have started today, then choose a bear which looks how you are feeling right now."

Neil looked around at what the others were doing and could see them taking this seriously. He then examined the cards carefully and picked one up.

"Can I go first?" asked Philip (13). Philip had been a member of the group for two terms. *"Of course!"* was my response but it wasn't needed because others in the group said the same thing.
"I felt OK really, but I was thinking about it a lot before the first Saturday, wondering what it would be like and if the other people would be friendly or if they might be a bit weird. I like it here, though!" said Philip, looking around at everyone in the circle before adding with a grin on his face, *"You are not weird, by the way!"*
"I can't remember how I felt," said Barry (13), who was a longstanding member of the group, *"but I do like the biscuits!"* Barry still found it difficult to express his feelings. Barry's comment about the biscuits (one he used regularly) was followed by forced laughter before he added, *"But I don't just come for the biscuits."* Iain (15) was the next to speak. *"It's a long time ago now, but I know I was anxious and I can remember being very shy and not being able to speak. I was a lot needier then! I'm more grown up now."*

Nathaniel (15) was the next to say his piece, holding his card up for everyone to see. Nathaniel had also been coming to the group for a long time and had formed a strong bond with Iain.

"I was the same as Iain," he began, glancing over to him with a smile, *"I felt I didn't need to come, though. I felt it wouldn't be much help. It made me angry at first and I got mad at my mum for bringing me. But I have made friends here and that's why I still come."* Neville (14), also a longstanding member, agreed with Nathaniel and added, *"Yes I felt anxious and nervous at first, but it's great now!"*

"I felt really nervous," added Belinda (14), the only girl in the group. *"I've been in groups at school before where the boys were horrible. There are a lot of boys here but I like all of you!"* Isaac spoke next. He was 13 and had been very quiet when he started the group a year earlier. He was much more confident and forthcoming now. *"I like you being in the group, Belinda,"* he said, *"You always say such interesting things and you are such a positive person."* Belinda giggled and thanked Isaac. He then picked up his card showing a very angry looking bear.

"When I first came," he said showing everyone his card, *"I felt really angry with my parents, a bit like Nathaniel felt. They told me I had to come and I wasn't allowed my opinion. They said I had no choice. I really didn't want to come. But when I got here I liked it and I still do. It's the best thing I do at the weekend."*

It was now Neil's turn. I had been watching him as the others spoke and he smiled and slightly nodded each time. It was as though each of the group had articulated his own uncertain feelings. Neil also witnessed how open the children could be with one another, how they could talk about uncomfortable feelings and be accepted. Neil seemed to be genuinely interested in what was going on. He had chosen a picture of a rather nervous looking bear. *"I felt nervous about coming today,"* he began, *"I didn't know what would happen. But it feels better now."*

By the end of the session, Neil looked more relaxed and said he would be happy to return the following week. He didn't tell his parents this, but such reticence is common. Neil's parents guessed it had gone well because the following Saturday he didn't complain and was dressed and ready without prompting.

Not all first sessions turn out as calmly as this, but this particular group was well established and they trusted and liked one another, having shared many ups and downs together. Neil was feeling the benefits of them being able to talk openly with each other about their vulnerabilities. What is interesting is that a group is not just a collection of individuals: it becomes an entity in itself. As the group develops and matures, members who are less mature grow emotionally and rise to the maturity of the group. This is what happened to Neil, and he quickly settled into this group.

When a child has not been properly prepared before starting a group

There was one occasion, when I failed to properly prepare an 11-year-old boy for the group; he didn't manage to settle and gave up after the first session. His story gives a strong message to us all about the importance of preparation.

GORDON'S STORY

Gordon's parents had been waiting for a place to become available in the group, but in the meantime had asked for some counselling sessions for the whole family. Gordon had a younger sister, who was nine. The work was going well and after three family sessions Gordon seemed to begin to trust me. His parents had not told him about the group, nor had they said he might join it. I hadn't realised this, but nor had I talked about the group during the family sessions as I thought it would be some time before a place became available. We had been working on family issues.

When a place came up in a group unexpectedly, the day after the third family session, and it was a group which I felt would be ideal for Gordon (because of his age and my knowledge of the other group members), I offered it to the family and his parents enthusiastically accepted. Unfortunately there was no time for Gordon to make an individual visit before that first Saturday, so he was not given a chance to hear or express his feelings about the group. In other words he had not been given the usual preparation that other children normally have. His parents and I arranged for him to come without consulting him first. He found it impossible to speak during the session and simply refused to return when he was reunited with his parents at the end of the session. We could not persuade him to change his mind and I felt it was important to respect his feelings.

Since then, I have thought about what happened and wonder if I was responding to a hidden dynamic within the family, which was to ignore or to over-ride Gordon in some way. Maybe we were all acting out this hidden dynamic and didn't realise it at the time.

However, one learns from mistakes. I am now very clear with parents about the importance of the initial visit. We make sure that every child, since Gordon, meets one of the team first to hear about the group and has the opportunity to say how he or she feels about joining. Any reservations or concerns can be acknowledged, thought about and talked through.

THINGS TO THINK ABOUT

I wonder if you recognise yourself in this chapter. Maybe you are a parent who would like your child to join a group, but aren't sure how it might be helpful. Maybe you work with children and are wondering how to start a group? Probably the most important thing to think about first is the way you prepare a child before they start any group (and this could be Brownies, football, drama or even a new school) so that they aren't overwhelmed by anxiety.

The next most important thing is for there to be a good working relationship between a parent and the group leader or leaders. You both need to trust each other. And the third thing is to show the child you have confidence in them and in the group working for them.

CHAPTER 4

The session framework - the six rhythms

Like all creative enterprises, the Friendly Group has developed organically and has settled into a successful framework with six rhythms. The rhythms I describe here are not intended as a prescriptive way of working but rather as a containing structure for a group of children. The groups are made up of six to eight children within a two to three year age range. Children can attend a group from ages eight to sixteen years. Usually there are eight children in a group. There is a group leader and two support facilitators who are usually teachers or therapists. The sessions last for one hour and ten minutes: most children arrive in those first ten minutes before the formal start and settle in by playing with the resource materials or talking to the adults.

The six rhythms

In this chapter you'll read about what the rhythms involve, what resources I use and how children often respond to them. There are two separate chapters (5 and 11) to describe *Circle Time with the Stone* and the *Story* in more detail. The other rhythms are explained more fully here and are also illustrated by the stories that appear throughout the book. I've used the term 'rhythm' because I feel it captures the gentle flow between the different parts of the session.

I hope the descriptions of the rhythms we use in the Friendly Group will give you some ideas about what might work for you, if you are planning to run your own group with children and young people. However, even if you are a parent, you may find that you can adapt some of the ideas for home. What I have found is that having the routine of the rhythms seems to help children and young people to think about and process their emotions, reduce their anxiety and relate better to others. These are the six rhythms.

- **Circle Time with the stone**
- **Bear Cards**
- **Creating a group story**
- **Choosing time**
- **Circle Time**
- **Lighthouse goodbye**

Each rhythm allows for spontaneity, reflection, creativity and development, with the focus of the whole session being about working in the *here-and-now* rather than the *then-and-there*. This means that the adults facilitating the group actively respond to what the children bring to the group (the emotional and relational dynamic) as the session unfolds on any particular day.

As I have said elsewhere, this isn't a social skills group per se and the children are not following a structured programme or curriculum. There is no teaching or instruction in the traditional sense of the word. The Friendly Group is also different from a strictly psychotherapeutic group in that the adults offer some structure and guidance within the sessions. Rather like Kurt Hahn's philosophy of Outward Bound (Hogan 1968), the children are impelled into experiences and reflections through the opportunities that are offered to them.

The rhythms are simple and open ended but, because they are within a contained and predictable framework, the children feel safe and are able to respond and learn. As the Friendly Group is a 'slow open' group, there will always be a core (and usually the majority) of children who have already been members for a while. We find that it works well to invite one of the 'old handers' to describe to a newcomer what happens during the session. This is often done by going through the framework, which is presented as an illustrated poster, hung on the wall. Their descriptions are often delivered virtually word for word in the way we explained it to them in the first place!

1   Circle Time with the stone

I was first introduced to the idea of Circle Time by my late colleague, Arthur Jordan, when I was working for Surrey Educational Authority in the late 1980's. He was always on the look out for new ways that educational psychologists could support teachers in schools and in 1989 showed me an article written by Murray White in the *Times Educational Supplement* about Circle Time. In this article White described how Circle Time not only promoted positive self esteem, but also increased children's levels of motivation and success in learning.

Essentially Circle Time is a dedicated time where children sit on the floor in a circle and each has a turn to speak without any interruption. The rest of the group listens. Children can share their experiences, views and feelings in this safe space, knowing they will not be judged or criticised. The very act of speaking, feeling heard, understood and taken seriously are all at the heart of any therapeutic process. However, when that happens in a group it is not only beneficial to the individual speaker, it also serves to increase the bond in a group and to facilitate future co-operation and engagement in the learning environment. This process feels both ephemeral and spiritual: no wonder Murray White (2009) describes it as 'magic' in his wonderful book called *Magic Circles*. However we're not promoting spirituality in a formal sense. What we want is to promote acceptance, connection and belonging. We use a special stone to indicate who the current speaker is (*see* Chapter 5).

2 Bear Cards

The next rhythm is entitled *Bear Cards,* a resource which facilitates the possibility of thinking and talking about feelings in a non-threatening way. In March 2003 I had the good fortune to be introduced to the *Bear Cards* at a workshop led by an Australian therapist, Russell Deal, who had developed the set of forty eight resource cards for use with families. I could see immediately these cards as having very positive and stimulating application potential for the Friendly Group. I have not been disappointed.

The set of cards have forty eight illustrations of single bear characters of different sizes using both facial expressions and body language to convey a wide range of emotions without words. They are about the single most useful resource that I have (*see* **Appendix** *for full details*). We use them with parents, teenagers and children on their own or in family groups as well as in the Friendly Group. Parents have even borrowed them and tried using them at home. They allow us to begin to think and talk about feelings in a gentle 'third person' way. It can be easier to say *"The bear is feeling worried"* than *"I am feeling worried"*. When working with families or individuals a card can be looked at together, reducing the pressure of making direct eye contact. It allows for other feeling words to be introduced and to help extend a child's vocabulary from the basic *happy, sad* and *angry*.

The same principle is applied to groups, where the card creates a bridge between the child and the feelings expressed. Each participant has a chance to say how the bear is feeling and to tell their story, if they wish. I invite others to share if they have felt the same way, allowing not only the speaker to reflect on their own experiences but for the rest of the group to be able to begin to relate to others through their shared experiences. Some children find it so difficult to express their feelings in the group, that simply showing the card is as much as they can do. However, by doing even just that, they are opening themselves up, which allows other children to respond and make connections with them. *"I know how you feel"* may be the first time a child has expressed empathy.

This can then be taken further by inviting the children to share, *"What does it feel like, right now, to be telling the group these things?"* or *"I wonder how it feels to find out that someone else in the group feels the same way as you?"* This enables the group to work in the *here-and-now* which I describe in more detail in Chapter 6 (*Group process*).

Below are some of the introductions that help children to talk about their feelings. They are set out in no particular order. A fuller set can be found in the Appendix at the end of this book.

> **PICK UP A BEAR WHO LOOKS LIKE YOU FEEL ...**
> - when you feel someone is bullying you or someone else you know
> - when someone in the group is behaving in a way you don't like
> - about going to a new school and leaving an old one
> - about leaving the group / about 'so-and-so' leaving the group
> - when someone listens to you and takes you seriously
> - when something bad has happened (like you've been in a fight, lost something or felt frightened)
> - when you feel forced to do something
> - when something good happens

In later chapters, you'll read not only how the children have responded to some of these introductions, but also how the adults have facilitated the flow of the discussion and sharing. It's often the timing, the wording and the tone of voice of the adult that helps the children take those tentative steps towards being able to talk about their own feelings and feel and show empathy towards others.

During this part of the session we sometimes use the *Worry Bear* instead of the

Bear Cards. A small teddy bear is placed in the centre of the circle and the children can choose to share a worry with the group. There is more detail about how this is used in Chapter 9.

3 Creating a story together

In this part of the session the children have the opportunity to *create a story* together. A story can be created during a single session or over several weeks. The ideas need to link together so the story makes sense. Each child has a turn to contribute an idea, which follows on from the previous child's contribution and is written down by one of the adults. The children can be free and creative without having the labour of doing the writing themselves. However, they can draw pictures if they want to. The finished story is typed up and given to the children in book form at the end of a set of sessions. The children can then re-read what they have created. The connections they have made with other children can be experienced again and again through their narrative.

I use this rhythm because the ability to create a narrative is the beginning of being able to think and process feelings and experiences in a safe way. The stories also give clues about how the children might be feeling but are unable to express and share in an open way. For example, monsters often crop up in the stories they create. Children all know about monsters; they are cold blooded creatures who have no feelings for those whom they are tormenting. Children dread having to face that monster, which might be a metaphor for facing scary adults in their lives or for facing the monstrous and ruthless qualities in themselves.

During the session established members are invited to explain to newcomers how the group creates stories. This is how Andrew (10) explained it.

> *"We always make up a story and it's often a quest,"* he began. *"We take turns to say our ideas and the first thing we usually do is choose what things*

to take. Sometimes we choose what we're going to wear. Our stories are always about going on a journey; sometimes we go by boat, sometimes in a spacecraft, sometimes on a magic carpet. We can decide!"

"Can we imagine anything we like?" asked Steve (11), who was new to the group. *"Yes we can!"* replied Andrew.

"But what if other people don't like my ideas?" asked Howard (9) in a quiet and rather timid sounding voice. It was Howard's first session too.

The group was then reassured that the grown-ups make sure that everyone has a chance to say their ideas and that we find a way to agree with one another. I have noticed that it's during the story part of the session when particularly anxious or shy children manage to find their voices. I remember one girl, who was a selective mute for the greater part of the session, but was able to use her voice with expression and enthusiasm for the story.

When the children create these stories together it can be the first time that they have made any links with others of their own age. It helps them to think about and experience feelings beyond themselves. I have written about the group story in more detail in Chapter 11.

TAKING ONE'S TURN IN THE STORY

In principle, when the children volunteer their ideas for the story, they can do so in whatever order or however many times they like. However, in the main, the children take single turns in telling their part of the story. In order to contain the children's anxiety, the order in which the children speak is negotiated and clearly written on paper. When a child has had their turn a line is drawn through their name. This is yet another example of how safe boundaries are put in place in the group. The fact that the children's names are written down with a number beside them and then crossed out once the children have said their piece gives a clear and reassuring prompt.

4 Choosing time

The name of this rhythm was coined by the very first group, when the youngsters requested a break, part-way through the session. During this part of the session the children have a chance to withdraw or be with the others and generally relax from the demands in the circle. They might play with toys (lego, large bricks, cars and so on) or with the outside play material (trampoline and trolley). They might simply walk around the garden area on their own. They sometimes draw, read, play the piano or talk with another child or adult. Drinks and biscuits are offered and when a child has a birthday there is always a little party with a cake. For many children this is the first time they have had a party or lit and blown out candles in the company of peers outside the family.

This is an interesting part of the session because the security of the circle is no longer there, and the adults have to split up to ensure there is support and supervision both inside and outside. An adult may have a conversation with one or more of the children. This is a different role from being an adult leader in the circle. However, it's good if the adults can stand back and allow the children to begin to play and socialise more independently. It also allows the adults to observe how the children relate to each other as they might do if they were at school or at home.

While the security of the circle boundary is no longer there, there are other boundaries and routines that offer security. There are the physical boundaries of the indoor and outdoor spaces. The trampoline and the trolley are contained spaces, and there are rules about how they might be used. These two are such important resources that I have written a chapter just about them (Chapter 10). Each child has their own cup with their name on it, hand-written on a paper label. The same drinks and biscuits are always offered in the same jugs and on the same tray. There is also the time boundary (of probably no more than five to ten minutes) and the children are always given a couple of minutes' warning about this part of the session coming to an end.

It is often in *choosing time* when friendships and social skills are tentatively explored. Mishaps and upsets can occasionally occur too, when someone feels hurt or angry with someone else's behaviour, usually as a result of a misunderstanding. You will read about some of these occasions in the stories told in later chapters.

5   Circle Time

At the end of the sessions there is another *Circle Time*, which offers the opportunity for reflection about what has happened over the past hour. It gives the children a chance to think and talk about how they have felt about themselves and other children in the session. They can re-visit those moments of connection, the small acts of kindness and their experiences of playfulness and humour. It often starts with one of the adults saying something like:

The 'sparkly moment' is the most open-ended invitation and also the one that triggers some of the children and young people's most interesting insights about themselves.

"I know it sounds odd that this is the best bit of the session, but it was when we were talking about bullying. How can talking about something so horrible make you feel so good afterwards? But it does! I feel so much happier now."
Claude (14)

"My sparkly moment was when we were talking about our worries. It's good to know that other people understand how I feel."
Sam (10)

"My sparkly moment was having fun when I was playing on the trampoline with Gareth and Rory."
Digby (11)

6 Lighthouse goodbye

One of the main challenges faced by children on the autism spectrum is coping with transition. In other words, it means coping with the end of one thing and the beginning of another. Transition triggers feelings of uncertainty, *"What will happen now?"* or emotional overload, *"I can't bear the feelings about having to get out of bed, finish my game, take off my clothes, put on my shoes, get into the car…"* and so on. What can happen is that children simply 'freeze and withdraw' or go into a 'meltdown'. This is where the rhythms of the session create familiar and safe boundaries to help process those transitions. There is predictability; *"We do this and then we do that."* So it was very important to create a ritual for the end of the session that would help the children and young people make the transition from being in the group to re-uniting with their families.

For this part of the session, one of the children places a model of a lighthouse in the centre of the circle. This is how we explain to a new child our ritual of saying goodbye to one another.

"A lighthouse has lights with beams that go round and round helping the ships pass safely by. Our eyes are like lights. Each of us will have a turn to say goodbye with our eyes, wishing each person a safe journey home and a safe time till we meet again."

The routine nature of this silent and peaceful ending allows the children to bring their emotional arousal down to a manageable level so they are able to leave calmly. It's interesting that even the children who struggle with eye contact in usual social situations are able to do this exercise and enjoy it.

A FINAL WORD

As groups mature and become settled and familiar with one another and as the children mature with age, so they can become more relaxed with the timing and the detail of the rhythms. The sessions develop an easy flow about them, not like a planned lesson. There can be occasions, for example, when there has been such intense discussion during the *Bear Cards* that the youngsters are happy to move straight into *choosing time* and miss out on *creating the story*.

Also the *story* part of the session itself evolves as a group evolves. In time the youngsters are ready to work in other ways during this part of the session, such as doing role-play or other activities that offer a creative outlet for expressing feelings or simply discussing a story that is read or told by one of the adults.

However, I feel that it is really important that time is always secured for an unhurried beginning and ending. It is the clear boundary that wraps round the whole session, offering the reliability and predictability that the children need to feel safe each time they come.

THINGS TO THINK ABOUT

In this chapter we've looked at the Friendly Group rhythms that make up the framework of a session. They work well for my colleagues and me. If you are planning to run a group you might like to try out any of them to see if they might work for you. Indeed you might want to create the same (or similar) framework for yourself.

If you are a parent, you might like to adapt some of these ideas at home. Many families have very successfully created their own versions of *Circle Time with the Stone* at family mealtimes, though not necessarily using an object to hold. Simply giving each member of the family a turn to speak without interruption creates a special space for everyone. In families where there is a lot of anxiety and negativity (and you may yourself be going through a rough time) it can be very affirming to take turns saying something positive about each member.

Circle Time with the stone

Circle Time with the stone is the first rhythm of the session framework. We've found it an excellent way to begin as the process is both predictable and calming. Everyone is invited to sit on the cushions which are arranged on the floor in a circle. One of the adults holds the stone and sits quietly till the children have settled themselves. The atmosphere soon has a feel of the beginning of a meditative practice. There may have been wriggling, laughing and talking beforehand but once the stone is picked up a sense of mindful awareness follows, and the children are immediately quiet.

The symbol of the circle

Aniela Jaffe (1978) says of the circle,

> Whether the symbol of the circle appears in primitive sun worship or modern religion, in myths or dreams, in the mandalas drawn by Tibetan monks, in the ground plan of cities, or in the spherical concepts of early astronomers, it always points to the single most vital aspect of life - its ultimate wholeness. p.266

Whilst the Friendly Group does not use the circle in any kind of religious sense, the symbol of the circle is universal. I like the fact that sitting in a circle substantially reduces any feeling of hierarchy as everyone is equally placed. There is a sense of togetherness and inclusion. The circle itself creates a safe boundary and a containing space within. It's also a reflection that the group is part of a larger whole and not something small and separate.

All over the world people gather together in circles. Even many governmental buildings now work on the basis of arranging the seating in a circle (like the European parliament). Many old churches in England are being modernised on the inside with the rows of pews being replaced with chairs that can be arranged in circles.

The symbol of the stone

During the *Circle Time* part of the session, the children pass around a stone. When they are holding it, it is their turn to speak. von Franz (1978) describes how the Self (our sense of who we are) can be symbolised in the form of a stone:

> Perhaps crystals and stones are especially apt symbols of the Self because of the 'just-so-ness' of their nature. Many people cannot refrain from picking up stones of a slightly unusual colour or shape and keeping them, without knowing why they do this. It is as if the stones held a living mystery that fascinates them. [People] have collected stones since the beginning of time …
>
> <div align="right">p.221 <i>my parantheses</i></div>

I am one of those people who can't resist picking up pebbles and stones! My collection has mainly come from beaches. In 1984, I found a wonderful pebble on Charmouth beach on the Jurassic coast in Dorset. What appealed to me wasn't its colour, a dull grey, but its smooth texture and oval and slightly uneven shape together with the fact it has three holes. At the time, the stone had the properties of a rattle because it is hollow and housed a small fossil, which made a delightful sound when I shook it. When I started working with groups, this stone seemed the ideal object which children could hold when it was their turn to speak. However, one day the little fossil got worn away with the shaking and fell out of one of the holes. It is now a silent stone, but the little holes and indention look remarkably like the features of a face, which also appeals to the children who handle it.

It's my choice to use a stone: but any small object that can be held in the palm of the hand could be used for *Circle Time*. The important thing is to use the same object for each session.

Guidelines for Circle Time with the stone

Below is the way I introduce the guidelines for this part of the session.

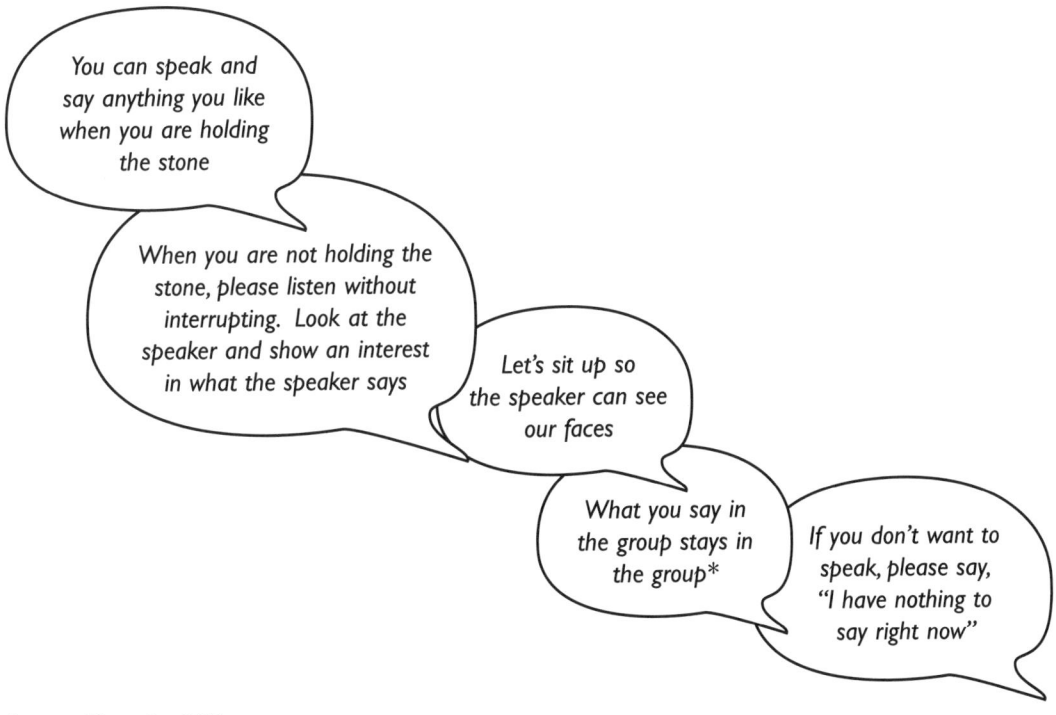

*see p.48 and p.205

The *Circle Time* offers space for each child to simply be able to speak for themselves and to be heard; it is not the time for discussion.

We make a point of explaining that listening involves being active; that it is positively doing something. It was Carl Rogers who developed the idea of 'active listening' in his therapeutic work in the 1960s. At first, many children interpret listening as simply a matter of 'not' talking, reverting to the negative and an experience of restraint. We usually say something like;

> *When you don't have the stone you can give the person who is speaking a good feeling by listening to what they are saying and showing interest in what they have to say*

Sometimes a child forgets what he wants to say when the stone reaches him. It can be as a result of suddenly 'being in the spotlight'. It can be simply due to the long wait or because he has become distracted with what others have been saying. Whatever the reasons, the 'forgetting' can trigger anxiety. The child then needs time to recollect his thoughts. Any uncomfortable feelings are acknowledged by the adults. We might say,

> *I can see that you are feeling frustrated and that makes remembering even more difficult. Just take your time. We can wait*

Occasionally a child will invite comments from others when they have the stone, but this is discouraged. If a child finds it difficult to speak or can't think of anything to say, then they are invited to say the following to the group.

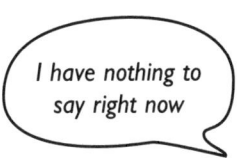

An example of Circle Time with the stone

This is an example of actual comments made during one session, which took place with a group of nine to 12-year-olds. The sentences are unrelated as the children were each sharing whatever was important to them that morning. As I've just said, this isn't a discussion. The subject matter ranged from future plans, reflections on the week, 'showing something' and expressing feelings.

(E) "I'm really excited because I am going to Cornwall soon for my holiday. I love it there because there are big waves."

(W) "It was strange this week because when I let my dog Lily out in the garden she did not run round as usual. She just stood still and looked at the sky. She was staring at the sky for ages. A bit later there was a big storm."

(J) "I've brought this lego model that I made to show you. I will pass it round so you can all see it. You can play with it at choosing time if you like but you have to be careful because it's very delicate."

The model was passed round and briefly looked at by everyone. When it reached J again he then handed the stone to N.

(N) "I've had a good week. At school I built a moving toy with one of my friends. By the way, we are going to move into the new school building soon. It is nearly finished."

(D) *"I have very bad hay fever so it's difficult to talk. I hope it goes away because it's my birthday soon and I am having some friends round for a party."*

(H) *"It is lovely to be here! I like seeing everyone. It's sunny and that means we can play on the trampoline. I like that … and it was my auntie's birthday recently."*

(K) *"I've got nothing to say."*

(L) *"Last night I had a really bad dream. In my dream there was a man staying in the house and he started to do mean things to me. I tried to escape from him. It was really frightening as dreams feel very real to me."*

This comment immediately triggered a reaction within the group and E and H put up their hands. L said they could speak.

(E) *"People in bad dreams feel like they're real and like they are in your room. When that happens to me I put sheets over my head."*

(H) *"I went to a sleepover once and had a nightmare when I was sleeping in Bill's room. It was very scary."*

The adults acknowledged that dreams are sometimes scary and L was asked how he felt about telling us about his dream.

(L) *"I feel a lot better."*

Bringing up difficult issues and bringing in objects

Children have talked about a whole range of subjects over the years, including their worries about such things as being bullied, the death or serious illness of a family member and the anxiety around exams or school transitions. Sometimes an immediate response is required. At other times these disclosures are worked on in more depth using the *Bear Cards*, which I describe in Chapter 4.

> **THINGS TO THINK ABOUT**
>
> The purpose of this first rhythm is to help children settle down together at the start of the session. By 'checking in' and telling their stories (or not), we the group leaders can gain a sense of not only how individual children are feeling on that day but also the general feel of the group as a whole. We tune in to the children's levels of emotional arousal. Are they excitable, quiet or agitated? Do any of them seem particularly withdrawn? Are any of them in a particularly light-hearted or positive mood?
>
> By paying attention to these things we can more effectively work on what is called *group process*. In therapeutic terms this is when the leaders are making sense of the here-and-now feelings and experiences and helping the children to think and talk about them as they are happening. I've devoted the whole of the next chapter to describing what *group process* is because it is at the heart of the therapeutic experience. It is what makes the Friendly Group different from a social skills group where the focus is usually on teaching skills.

CHAPTER 6

Group process: working in the here-and-now

The potency of group process

Parents are often baffled by the intensity of enthusiasm their children express about coming to the group. They say things like,

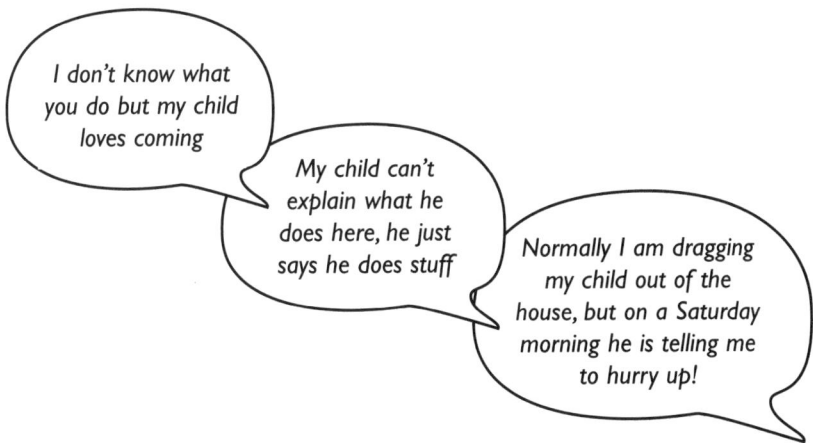

One of the main reasons for the children's enthusiasm is because we are offering a safe and unhurried environment in which to help them begin to reflect a little about their feelings. The children usually find it very difficult to talk about feelings, especially uncomfortable ones, like anxiety, fear and distress. Feelings can build up inside them and burst, almost without warning like a pressure cooker, into a 'meltdown.' However, when children are supported through the *process* of the group, to begin finding ways to express their thoughts and feelings, they are taking their first steps towards not only learning how to regulate or manage their emotions but also discovering what it feels like to make connections with others, who might feel the same way.

During the sessions we are not working from 'typical scenarios' taken from a text book or manual. The children are not being directed into theoretical discussions about what emotions look like or how to behave in certain situations. We are instead working on understanding what is happening between the children and ourselves on any particular day. Also, instead of simply attending to *what* is being said, or *how* the children are behaving, which in therapeutic language is called the *content*, we are focusing on *process*, making sense of the 'here-and-now' feelings and experiences *about* what is happening (Yalom and Molyn 2005).

For example if a child (let's call him Howard), says in front of the group that he has been bullied, one of the adults might say to the whole group,

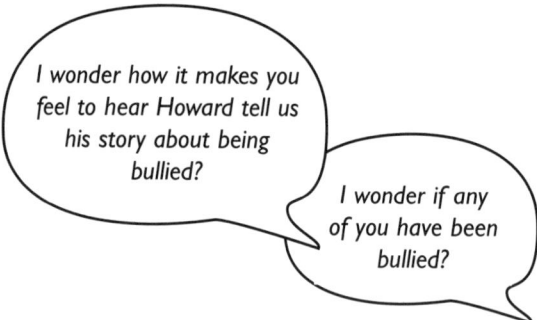

This brings the children into the present moment; they are being invited to think about their own feelings. However they might become quite agitated by this. Some children might retreat by going under the table, behind the curtain or opening up a book. There are others who might distract themselves from their own discomfort by throwing objects or making inappropriate comments, such as commenting on the appearance of one of the group members. Other children may seem sympathetic but they can unwittingly block group process by offering advice. At a superficial level, advice can look positive, but when children offer advice it usually indicates their own discomfort and defensiveness. It is easier to focus on someone else's struggles than on their own difficulties. It should also be said that the children may also want to offer advice to help them feel better because they want resolution and to resolve something creates a greater feeling of certainty. *"If this worked for me then it should work for you."*

However, if children are able to openly express their vulnerable feelings and share their own experiences of, let's say, being bullied, the group suddenly feels very alive. This is because relational connections are being made. The adults help the children to see this by saying things like,

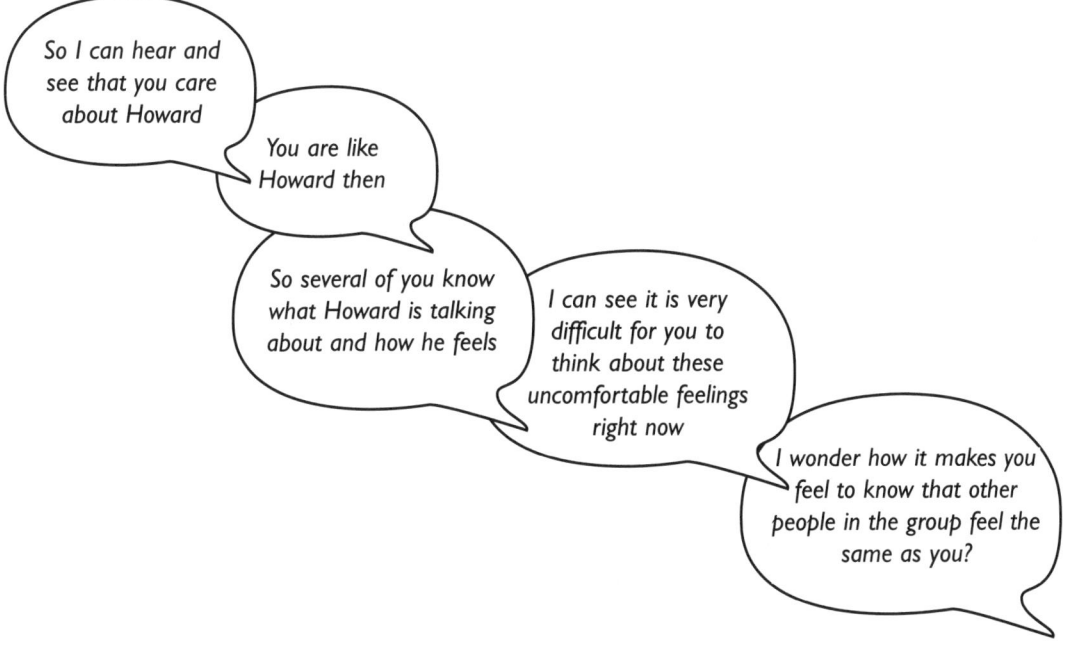

These types of comments, questions and 'wonderings aloud' help the children and young people yet further in their development. This will become clearer as you read about the children's stories.

Over time the group develops a bond, because they have jointly created memories which are threaded together and become part of the *'group history'*. The memories may be talked about in the future, creating further strengthening of the group bond and opportunity for learning.

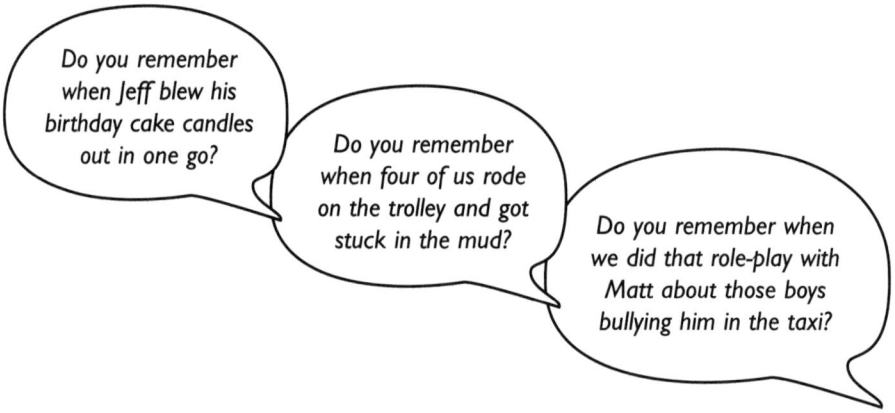

In summary, the potency of the group process comes from the leaders -

- attending to what is called 'dynamic administration', which is making sure that the room and resources are ready and reliably the same each week
- recognising that they are active members of the group and are also affected by what goes on in it
- noticing and gently drawing attention to the behaviour of the children and young people and how they might be feeling by 'wondering aloud' about what might be happening
- being flexible, alert and observant

- helping the children to share their feelings and to notice how it affects themselves and others in the group
- bringing this awareness to the *group as a whole*
- guiding the children towards noticing the connections that are being made between themselves and others
- Being able to 'step back' and be mindful that the behaviour expressed in the group is a mirror of how we all behave outside

Difficulties with working in the 'here-and-now'

Although I have described a little about working in the *here-and-now*, it is more difficult to put into practice than you might think. This is because the way children behave triggers feelings in all of us. You will feel empathy for some but may struggle to feel empathy for others. You might recognise aspects of yourself in the children or young people which you like or dislike (or may not even be consciously aware of). We all have the capacity to feel and behave like children at times. It is also worth being aware that getting caught up in the *content* (for example when a child goes on too long in telling a story about themselves), can slow down progress and development. Below are some typical behaviours and scenarios (*content*) that can take the leader away from attending to the here-and-now feelings (*process*).

DISTRACTING BEHAVIOUR

It is easy to get swept away and distracted, like other group members, by a dominant personality who is behaving in an attention-seeking way. When I say attention-seeking, this can carry negative connotations, but I don't mean to convey a negative message here. Everyone needs attention, but if the right kind of attention is not being given by the adults then the child might repeat the behaviour over and over again. It is as if the child is provoking the adult to understand their feelings and deliver the right kind of attention. The trouble is that while the behaviour goes on, others in the group may become irritated and either quietly tolerate the behaviour or copy it. Examples of distracting behaviour might include repeatedly butting in, querying what has been said, going on and on, wriggling, moving about and throwing things, making noises and touching other children. There can also be the passive attention-seekers, like the children who sit under the shelf, behind the curtain, lie on the floor, withdraw into another room or retreat within their clothing (like pulling coats or hoods over their heads). If the leader simply responds to the behaviour by telling the child to behave differently, then that is what it means to get *caught up in the content*. The behaviour has become a distraction *away from* thinking and talking about feelings.

GIVING COMPLIMENTS

Sometimes it feels right to express pleasure about a child in some way, such as a new haircut or the way he has been playing well with other children. It can stimulate feelings of pleasure in the child. However, if personal comments about things like social behaviour or appearance are *uninvited*, that child might feel as if he has been put in the spotlight and the emotional defences could go up. The child might become un-cooperative or start behaving in a provocative or 'silly' manner and you might find yourself pre-occupied with the child's behaviour (*the content*) rather then paying attention to how the child might be feeling (*the group process*).

BECOMING TOO INTERESTED IN CONTENT

One of the features of children on the autism spectrum is that they can be very knowledgeable about certain subjects and they can be very entertaining in the way in which they speak. Without realising it you can get interested in the narrative or simply enjoy being entertained. This can be appropriate for some of the time, but again, while the focus is on the narrative the attention is taken away from how the child might be feeling.

TALKING ABOUT A PAST EVENT

Occasionally I have invited a group to reflect on an experience of the previous week. What I have tried to do is catch up on a missed opportunity, but this isn't always possible. Invariably there is an immediate feeling of flatness. The children are trying to remember what happened. They have gone into 'thinking mode' rather than 'feeling mode'. They may not be able to recall how they felt. Some may not have even noticed this event at the time and so are unable to recall much at all. What then happens is that the talking can quickly turn into an intellectual exercise and the adults can slip into a 'teacher role', pointing things out or asking questions. Without the emotional impact of the here-and-now experience, the children can feel cut off from the talking and thinking and they learn very little from it. They might even describe it as boring. When the 'feeling mode' is activated this opens up the possibilities for making connections and this is *process*. Learning to make connections is the essence of therapeutic work.

Attending to the here-and-now

The immediate (here-and-now) events and feelings of the session need to be *noticed*. This means the adults have to be attentive 'moment by moment' to how the children are relating to one another; their behaviour and the way they express themselves. The adults also need to be prepared to go with the flow with what is unfolding, rather than rigorously trying to stick to any plans and structure. It also means being mindful of the children's past experiences that could be affecting their current behaviour and fuelling their emotions.

The here-and-now experience might be very exciting with many feelings expressed. However the experience alone will offer limited learning if the children in the group are not able to think about their feelings *at the time*. Another aspect is to share 'just happened' events and feelings so the experiences can be *thought about together*. As adults, we need to be attentive regarding the nuances of the children's behaviours and their comments, to be able to wait and to intervene at just the right moment. You need to be able to trust that the process will reveal itself, and that if you miss one moment then there are always second chances and you can be more attentive for the next moment. It's so easy to be hard on ourselves, when we recognise we could have intervened at a better time or in a better way. But recognising what we have missed can further heighten our attention for the future.

We need to understand that working with group process is a creative and open ended activity. Being a therapist is to be an artist, whose work is creative and open to interpretation. It's not about giving answers or being prescriptive about ways of behaving. It's about *wondering* and *finding ways of thinking and talking about* the behaviours and feelings that are being acted out and expressed during each session.

Making connections

At the end of one of the sessions, I invited the children to tell each other who they had noticed being kind or friendly that day. Sally was the first to speak. *"You have been kind and really sympathetic today, Toby."*

> *"I haven't been sympathetic,"* Toby replied with a puzzled tone of voice.
> *"I don't really understand what that means."*
> Sally continued, *"Well, when I was crying in choosing time, you came up to me and asked if I was alright. I felt a lot better after that because you'd noticed. That was you being sympathetic."*

Toby looked down, fiddling with a piece of Lego that was in his hands and took a moment or two to take this in. Then, lifting his head up and looking at Sally, before scanning the rest of the group, he said with a growing smile on his face, *"Well I guess I was sympathetic and didn't even realise it."*

The Friendly Group is a microcosm of life in the wider world

The way the children behave and relate to each other in a group is a mirror of what goes on elsewhere. The Friendly Group is like a microcosm of the social life they are experiencing outside. Knowing this, the sessions provide an opportunity for me and my colleagues to think about and better understand the children's strengths and difficulties. How the children express their pleasure, hurt, frustration and anxiety in the group tells us their ways of managing their feelings at home, in the classroom and in the playground.

Early on in the group, the children and young people can get stuck in their various defensive roles, such as being the *'loud mouth'*, *'quiet one'*, *'silly one'*, *'sarcastic one'* or *'the one who always has to go first'*. Maybe you recognise some of these in your own child or in the children you work with? What the children are doing is showing how they behave 'out there' and repeating it here in the group. The work of the group allows the children (when the time is right) to steadily unlock themselves from these defensive behaviours and thoughts, discovering other aspects of themselves and learning to behave in new ways. It's interesting that when the children create their own stories (which are part of the framework of the session) they often introduce the idea of using keys to unlock doors and portals and take them to new places. Sometimes a small shift can make a big difference to a child's happiness.

It is not just through conflicts and misunderstandings that the children learn about relationships and the part they play in relationships. Sometimes they express kindness or consideration for another, either verbally or through their behaviour and *do not realise it,* as was described in the interchange between Sally and Toby earlier. Through drawing attention to what has happened and encouraging the children to think a little, they have a here-and-now experience from which to learn. These experiences also serve as a rehearsal for how to express their feelings and relate to others outside the group. Time and time again the issues that come up within the group reflect the life issues that the children are facing outside, such as illness, loss, disappointment, shame, bullying, sharing, misunderstandings, loud noises and life transitions.

'Wondering aloud' stimulates 'working through'

When my colleagues and I *'wonder aloud'* with each other, we might say things like;

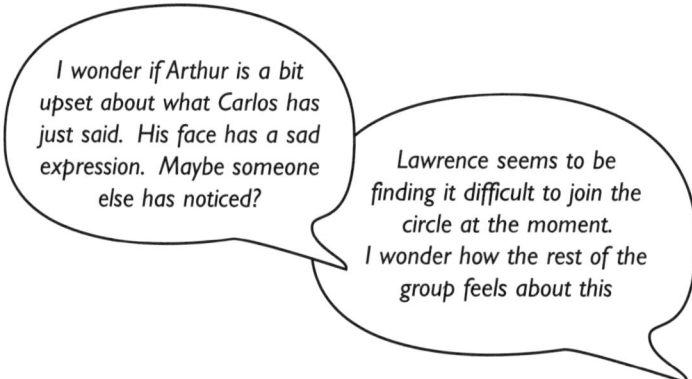

This *'wondering aloud'* is something open-ended and allows an imaginative response. There are no rights or wrongs or *"That's it"*. We are giving a narrative to the unfolding events and are giving words to the emotions the children might be feeling. What we are doing is not only giving voice to uncomfortable feelings in a safe and non-judgemental manner, but allowing associations to be made and imagination to develop. We are leaving things open, so more possibilities can be thought about and said. The imagination expands and life becomes richer.

Another vital role of *'wondering aloud'* is that of demonstrating to the children and young people what a good relationship can look like. The adults are modelling a positive way to talk and to listen to one another as they express care, concern, empathy and interest. It is also really important, when you are a child, to hear that adults are interested in you. It demonstrates that you are being thought about. You are someone who is noticed not just because of the way you behave on the outside but also because of how you might be feeling on the inside.

The group therapeutic experience is a communication process in which each child or young person learns how to share, explore and resolve problems with the leaders or other group members. It is a rehearsal for how to make relationships and deal with problems outside the group. Furthermore, the *youngsters experience* what it feels like to *belong* to something, to *fit in* with others similar to them and to *meet kindred spirits*.

THINGS TO THINK ABOUT

Children communicate how they are feeling through their behaviour. Over time habits form and children can get stuck in defensive behavioural roles. The behaviours can mask hidden aspects, for example aggressive behaviour can hide gentleness and emotional sensitivity. It is all too easy to focus on what a child has said or done without paying enough attention to his or her feelings. If you can guess how a child is (or might be) feeling from how they are behaving and then acknowledge those feelings, you will be helping them to think about their feelings and this in turn helps them to regulate them. What is more, children feel a greater connection with you because you have communicated that you understand them (or are trying to). It's *the intention of wanting to understand* that is what is so important.

Group process is when a group leader is able to help all members of the group to do this together. Group process works in a family group too. It's a wonderfully creative way of being with children and young people because you can go beyond the script of the 'all knowing' or 'authoritative' adult, and enter into a relational dance of emotional connection and understanding together.

CHAPTER 7

The leadership role

In group contexts for children and young people, there are several names for those who are in a leadership role. There are teachers in classrooms, coaches on a sports field, youth workers in a youth club and leaders in a scout or guide group. In the Friendly Group, I refer to myself and my colleagues as the adults, the grown-ups and sometimes as the leaders.

The leader as a musical conductor

Sometimes the leader of a group is called a *conductor* and I really like the term, because it describes the leadership role so well. It was Foulkes, the founder of Group Analysis, who first used the word conductor, suggesting that running a therapy group was more like conducting an orchestra than leading in the conventional, directive sense.

It is the role of a musical conductor to draw the music out of each individual musician to create something that is somehow greater than the sum of its parts. In a similar way, I see a kind of parallel in what happens in the Friendly Group. The adults conduct the rhythm and pace of the session; when to 'stay' with something that is being talked about and when to 'move on'. When an inexperienced orchestra is playing the music might bang and crash and become out of tune. So it can be with the children and young people: but as they work together, they become more in tune with each other. Ultimately it is the responsibility of the adults to help each child play their part so that the whole group can move towards harmony.

The leader as an electrical conductor

Another way of looking at the role is to describe the leader as a safe electrical conductor, who directs the emotional energy of the children to pass safely through. However, in order to become that safe conductor (that safe person) for the children, you need to be working on what is going on for you, personally; noticing how you are feeling, wondering about what's happening and asking yourself questions as the session unfolds. It's this ongoing process of self-reflection and questioning during the session that makes you a safe conductor of the group's energies.

In the Friendly Group, my colleagues and I are, if you like, the 'official' conductors. Children will transfer feelings they have had about other adults in the past, onto us. They might behave as if we were a grandparent, teacher or mother. When we notice and feel, for example, the energies of anger or distress being projected onto us, we calmly acknowledge that someone in the group might be distressed or angry and think about why that might be. We do this by 'wondering aloud' with each other and the children can hear our exchanges and know it is safe to be thinking about these things.

I WANT TO GO FIRST!

Often children get caught up in their feelings about what they want but are unable to think or talk about them (in other words, process them) and they simply act them out. For example, there have been times when a child, let's call him Jacob, has thrown an object at another member of the group in utter frustration, shouting, *"I want to go first!"* There is immediate heightened arousal from the other children (we can palpably feel the 'excitement' or 'anxiety') and it could be easy for us to simply focus on the 'content' of what has just taken place (the thrown missile) and comment on that, to bring the energy levels down. However, in so doing, it would take away the opportunity for Jacob and the rest of the group to think about and process their feelings, as we, the adults, would have simply taken charge. Instead, this is the kind of response I might make.

> *"I can see Jacob is getting angry because he wants to go first,"* I say aloud, looking at my colleagues. *"And Oscar says he wants to go first as well. It's difficult to know what to do when someone else is trying to have what you want. And it can make you feel angry."*
> *"Yes!"* agrees Jacob *"And I might forget what I want to say."*
> *"It's difficult when you are worried you might forget what you want to say,"* I continue, *"I wonder if anyone else knows that feeling?"*
> *"That's why I want to go first,"* says Oscar.
> *"I know that feeling,"* adds another member of the group.

Now the whole group is becoming involved and has a chance to think about and share their feelings with Jacob. What Jacob and the rest of the group might discover is that they all have desires to be first and that they can all worry about forgetting what they want to say. This kind of experience provides the opportunity for a child (and indeed for all the children in the group) to develop the emotional capacity of *pause* and *reflection*, enabling an aspect that is weak or even missing in them to be experienced; in this example, *patience, trust* and *tolerance*. This is when the emotional learning happens and children can begin to see that others have feelings like themselves. What is more; no-one is in the wrong. The scene continues.

> *"I wonder how you are going to sort out this problem,"* I query.
> *"You could play the 'scissors, paper, rock' game to decide,"* suggests another child, who explains the game.
> *"Okay! That's a good idea,"* agree Jacob and Oscar, both of whom are calmer now.

It may be that this game is acted out a few times till each party is satisfied, but the decision about who goes first will have been decided within the group and between the children themselves. Such an experience will then get remembered in the group. It will become a group memory about how they managed to resolve a problem together and may be brought up again in the future, further reinforcing good feelings of being part of the group.

This issue of 'who goes first' and turn-taking can be very difficult for a 'young' (in other words, newly formed) group or for a group where the children do not yet have the ability to think in this way, such as the less emotionally mature or those with more marked autism. In these groups I, as the leader, will suggest who will start and identify the direction of turn-taking in the circle. Alternatively, the order might be written down with the children's names against numbers 1-8 (if there are eight present). This offers clarity and boundaries to help the children feel calmer, knowing that they will have their turn. As the children and groups mature, greater flexibility evolves.

This is what I might say to Jacob and Oscar before they start to speak.

"I can see that you have sorted this out well between each other. It's not a good idea to throw things at someone in the group. It's much better to say if you are feeling angry about something. Well done to you, Jacob, for keeping calm."

In this way, the inappropriate behaviour has been talked about but without blame or shame, and I have been able to give some direction about an alternative way to deal with feelings of frustration.

And finally ... when working with children, the adult is in charge

The children and young people need someone who can offer clear boundaries, support and guidance. This doesn't mean being a prescriptive and authoritarian figure. It means being someone who is clear, strong, predictable, caring and stable and who will hold and contain a child's anxiety about the disturbances that will inevitably happen from time to time. The child can then begin the process of finding their own authority within and will eventually discover they can trust themselves without the need to look to a 'mummy figure' to take charge. To begin with, though, the children need guidance.

> *"It's alright, I am the grown-up and I am in charge,"* we will often say to a child who is trying to police others.
>
> *"I am here to keep you safe,"* is the reassuring phrase we use to indicate our leadership role.
>
> *"I understand this might be worrying you and you want to help but it is up to the grown-ups to deal with that,"* is another phrase we use to let a child know that they can rely on the adults.

The anxiety levels of some autistic children are so high that they can spend inordinate amounts of their time and energy trying to control what is going on around them, which gets in the way of their learning. In a group, when children begin to feel heard and understood by calm and responsive adults, it gives them the opportunity to relinquish some of that control, thereby easing the way for them to become more relaxed so they can develop and learn in their own time.

THINGS TO THINK ABOUT

Keeping children safe by being an adult who is strong about boundaries, support and guidance is relevant for both professionals and parents. However, let's not forget that when we're with children we will be picking up their feelings (and they ours: have you noticed, for example, that when you're feeling tired, children become more demanding?). Children's moods will affect not only our moods but also the strength of our resolve to keep to boundaries or our ability to be supportive and understanding.

It's essential we do stay in charge to help children feel safe. It's worth recognising the need for and the value of support from your peers. As a parent, this may be from your partner or other adult family relatives. It may be from a close friend or a support group. As a professional, it may be from your co-leader in the group or from a more senior colleague.

CHAPTER 8

Tension and turbulence

Sometimes there are disturbances in a group which can feel out of the leader's control. During a session for example, you might start to feel terribly anxious or even experience mild heart palpitations, which become so overwhelming that you become unable to think about what is going on. The overwhelming feelings of one (or more than one) child or teenager are not only being projected onto you, but are also getting inside you. So you are feeling these emotions *almost as your own*. You may even begin to behave in a defensive way yourself, mirroring some of the behaviours in the group. This can also happen if you unconsciously identify in others something about yourself that you don't like. This is what is termed *projective identification*.

When this happens, your capacity to think is being attacked; but so is everyone else's in the group too. Everyone is feeling something that is too frightening and difficult to be thought about, and it's this that creates the tension and disruptive behaviours in the group. Often one child might be singled out as the troublemaker, but what I have come to understand is that such a child is simply acting out the 'disturbance' for everyone else. What is more, the disturbance can feel like a challenge of one's authority and it takes professional experience and support from other colleagues to learn to distinguish between what are your own feelings and what 'belongs' to someone else. Disturbance is a common experience when working in a group, and although it can be deeply unsettling and perplexing at the time, it offers the opportunity to create movement, learning and development. A group needs something to 'chew on' for there to be vitality and growth.

However, it isn't just negative emotions that can create turbulence. You might find yourself feeling strangely positive or euphoric. Or you might feel unrealistically elated. If this kind of thing happens it's important to ask yourself why, otherwise you could find yourself feeling and acting a bit manic. Because these feelings can also come from members of the group, and we need to recognise this.

Making sense of turbulence in a group

When a group fails to connect or if there is some turbulence or chaos in the group it might be that some individuals have worries about belonging, fitting in or feeling worthwhile, and they create disturbances that trigger other people's similar worries. It might also be that members of the group don't trust that the adults will be able to demonstrate authority (being in charge) safely and calmly. When this happens it can be described as the group *being in regression*. When I talk about authority, I'm not talking about the simplistic notion of someone who 'waves the finger', as it were, or gives out punishments. I am talking about someone who is able to demonstrate that they can feel, think and act firmly, without crumbling in the face of challenge or disruption. In other words it is about being able to stand back while also still being fully present to what is happening.

I have discovered over time that there are several common ways that the children or teenagers might behave, which can create the kind of division or disruption I am describing.

- Challenging our authority as leaders is often demonstrated when children are struggling with being in charge of themselves. They might do this by saying that something we are doing is boring, or that we have 'done it before'. Another challenge is to simply be un-cooperative. When children behave in this way, they need to see you, the adult as being able to withstand these attacks. This is because if you are seen to survive them, then you act as a 'survivor' and a strong role model for them. At a deep level they will sense that they might learn this too, and be strong.

- Sometimes there is low level bullying such as sniggering, whispering, wise-crack comments, kicking and nudging. It might be that the youngsters are trying to vie for position in the group or express their awkwardness and insecurity.
- Some children talk and talk without a pause, but then become agitated and defensive if asked to finish off what they are saying. In some cases this might suggest that the other members of the group have made no impression on them. In other cases it might be that they are filling up the space leaving none for anyone else, in an attempt to be special; craving individual attention and recognition.
- There are also children who seem to be acting out, in a verbally inarticulate way, their own family dynamics, such as undermining another child (if they are being undermined at home), pushing boundaries or picking on a particular member of the group as a scapegoat.
- Cutting across when another person is speaking is another common behaviour. This might be achieved by throwing something across the room or through interrupting by changing the subject or with cutting remarks. This behaviour cuts across the mental and emotional links that are being made in the group. Children who do this may not know how to 'get in' to a group but want their presence felt. However, when connections are broken things become meaningless, because relationships are built on making connections with others.
- Repeatedly telling jokes can be disruptive too, and might be a child's way

to avoid thinking and talking about difficult feelings. However, in a well established group, where the children trust each other, the telling of a joke or engaging in banter can make a serious matter bearable. I have noticed this is particularly the case with groups of teenagers.

- Sometimes children publicly threaten to leave the group, suggesting there might be issues of rejection in their lives: they need to hear that the adults will not give up on them.

PROCESSING TURBULENCE

Below is an extract of some notes I made at the end of a session, as a way of processing my helpless and frustrated feelings, with one particular group of young teenagers. Whilst the writing did help to ground me and to release some of my tension, it wasn't until I reflected with my supervisor that my feelings and the youngsters' behaviour really made sense to me.

> *It was such hard work to keep the group together today and it has left me feeling empty. I felt they let me do all the work. I tried to be calm and relaxed but the atmosphere still became noisy and tense. The children weren't listening to each other. They were reverting to the old disruptive behaviours they exhibit when they feel stressed. One of them was taking charge and telling the others to be quiet. Another was whispering, making wise-crack comments and saying 'put downs' towards other group members. Jeremy was rolling around the floor, making faces, being argumentative and making inappropriate comments. No-one seemed to show any real interest in anyone else.*
>
> *I feel a sense of dread about seeing them next week. They don't feel like a group. They all seem like individual strangers bumping into one another. They have talked about bullying this term, and some have even relished telling the others how they don't care if they have been mean to someone who is bullying them. That sense of revenge as true*

> *justice was shared and accepted. Discussions about bullying over the internet became disturbingly intense and distorted. "Well it's only in fun and you don't know them, so it's not really bullying," were the arguments of a couple of the members. I could feel that this was unsatisfactory but the negative forces seemed to get a hold.*

Looking back on this in a supervision session, I wondered if my feelings were a reflection of what was going on inside the children. Their behaviour communicated feelings of disconnection, frustration, helplessness and emptiness, and I felt them too. None of the youngsters were feeling safe in the group and this was communicated to me. There were also a couple of twosome alliances. Such alliances can be divisive if they are not acknowledged by the whole group. On this particular occasion, instead of addressing the uncomfortable feelings within the group, I took them on as my own. It took time for me to realise and remind myself that I, too, was a member of the group just like the others. In attempting to regain my own sense of connection and control I tried to exercise control of the children by attempting to smooth over the disruptions instead of addressing how they felt (as a group) about them.

It is easy to feel a failure when things feel out of control or go wrong in a group but, as leaders, we can learn so much from these situations. The good thing is that you can always go back and help the group think and talk about their feelings another time. A group will usually respond and grow if difficult feelings are able to be thought and talked about with adults who are able to 'hold' them rather than absorb them. This particular group did think and talk about their feelings and went on to become a very supportive and cohesive group of teenagers.

Feelings of emptiness at the start of sessions

At the start of a set of sessions I have sometimes been aware of an initial feeling of emptiness. It is a kind of loneliness that you feel when you don't feel connected with others and these feelings can be a mirroring of what the children are feeling when they return to or start the group.

When I began working with groups, I didn't appreciate that even one new member turns a group into a 'new group'. Can you remember a time you first joined a group? Maybe it was a choir, a football club or even meeting new colleagues at the start of a new job? Can you remember that feeling of being the outsider? Can you remember the anxiety until you managed to talk to someone? When you make a link, even with only one other person, you feel more connected and part of the group and it becomes less terrifying.

Just imagine what it must be like for the children who come to the Friendly Group? They are children who find it particularly difficult to make those first links with others. Their weak social skills are painfully apparent to us, the adults, when the children fail to approach one another, or when they ignore another's approach, or when they make inappropriate personal comments or do not listen to one another. Some children butt in and make intrusive comments in the group. They want to make sure that someone will notice them and respond to them: even a negative response is better than no response at all. Such behaviours are clues that they may be acting out their primitive fears of being alone in this world. It's so important to remember that all children (indeed all of us) have a profound fear of being left out, excluded, dropped or forgotten. It is a nameless dread. The worst possible experience is to feel 'unwanted', 'invisible' or 'unnoticed' as if you don't exist, as if you are a 'nobody'… a 'no-thing'.

Dealing with rivalry - one group's story

This is the story of a mixed group of 10-12 year olds. The boys in the group had been together for some time, but two new girls (both 11-years-old) had only recently joined. They were all still finding their 'places' and were behaving in ways that reflected the difficulties they have outside the group. There was social clumsiness in the way they talked and played with one another, and the group felt disconnected and rather tense.

Jenna (11) attempted to take the lead role by using her own kind of 'psycho-babble' to explain people's behaviour and why they might be unkind. She came across as someone with 'all the answers'. Her lengthy narrative did not mean much to the others as the children did not know the school friends she was describing or the TV programme to which she was referring to illustrate her points. She had reverted to her 'expert mode', which was probably a form of defensiveness, and paid no attention to the rising restlessness in the other children as she went on and on.

Artem's (12) attempts to take the lead role withered as the others 'talked over' him. They interrupted each other, competing in their 'sob stories' and becoming over-stimulated. In this way they were severing their links between each other. Two of the others then went unusually quiet.

Cerys (11) played for the 'top dog' position through a provocative behavioural style of being loud and almost hysterical in the way she spoke. This was a far cry from the almost mute and timid demeanour she presented at the first session. It became particularly apparent during the part of the session when the children were making up a story together. The children tend to enjoy the *story* part of the session and I have written about the therapeutic value of this activity in Chapter 11. What happens in the story is often a reflection of what is happening in the group.

In this particular story Artem said that the group had been separated from their time machine by a dragon that flicked its tail and hurled them all miles away and into a jungle. Jenna then came up with the idea of finding a talking flower there. This flower gave a message about how the group could get back to their time machine. At this point Cerys continued the story by saying she was leading the group through a portal that would take everyone back in time. This is how Cerys continued the story;

> *'Cerys thought Jenna had been mean and this meanness had killed the flower. Would we be stuck here, back in time? Jenna had a meltdown about this and Artem was very sad because he loved the flower. Jenna decided to bury the flower but Artem began to dig at the earth with his keys and fell into the mud.'*

Cerys had, through the metaphor, unconsciously challenged the very two who rivalled her in becoming special as the 'top dog' member, by attributing her negative and humiliating feelings and behaviours to them. Past issues were being reworked through this story. I could see that Artem had become rigid in his body posture and was muttering under his breath; clues that his rage was about to burst. Not only did he like things to be orderly and clean, but he also did not openly express affection. The words that Cerys had used probably felt too threatening for him to cope with and looked as if they were about to overwhelm him.

The children needed adult help to process this and to resolve the impending crisis. I could see that at a conscious level Cerys didn't realise the impact that her words had had on Artem, nor had she noticed or read his body language. I wondered if she had got caught up in her own habitual need to take control in order to manage uncertainty. I have seen this often before in the Friendly Group, when children overstep the mark by being negative about someone else through seemingly humorous comments. As I have already said, this can be a form of unconscious attack that comes from a place of deep vulnerability and anxiety. It was at this point I stepped in. *"I wonder what the group thinks about today's bit of the story,"* I began.

This was the opening that Artem needed, because without hesitation, he said that he didn't like the flower bit. Artem needed some encouragement to say a little more about how it had troubled him. Jenna added (taking the text literally), that she didn't like the bit about her killing the flower as it was something she would never do. Interestingly she didn't mention the reference to her having a meltdown. It was as if the notion that she could hurt something touched her sensitive nature far more at that moment.

> *"I can understand that Cerys's ideas for the story have been upsetting,"* I continued. *"I wonder how you feel now that you have said something,"* I added, making eye contact with Jenna and Artem.

They both said they felt a bit better but still didn't like the last bit in the story. Cerys listened to this and was quiet for a few moments. I acknowledged that it was probably difficult for her to listen to these comments. I wondered if she now felt awkward and embarrassed. However Cerys demonstrated she had 'heard', and therefore empathised with the others' discomfort, when she offered a spontaneous and genuine apology, which was immediately accepted by Artem and Jenna. The palpable tension that had built up in the group was then released and the children were able to enjoy the *choosing time* part of the session.

This kind of behaviour, where children try to 'trip each other up' is a completely normal part of growing up. Cerys and the whole group needed to hear that I (the adult) was not shocked by what had been said and could give them a chance to work through it themselves in the session. All children and young people are mean to each other at times. Indeed we can all resort to cutting or cynical remarks or 'put down' banter at times.

The story had offered an opportunity for the rivalries to be expressed but it needed some adult guidance to help the children understand it a bit better. However, when I intervened, it was at the risk of shaming Cerys, which I didn't want to do. Because if Cerys had been given the role of the 'baddie' by the group, it would have had negative consequences. It would have created a feeling of hostility and the need for taking sides in the group. For Cerys, it could have become a deeply personal attack, bringing out her bad feelings about herself. She could have become withdrawn and defensive.

This was where my role as leader was so important. I had noticed Jenna and Artem's discomfort and the tension that was brewing in the group. I had noticed that neither Artem nor Jenna had been able to openly express their discomfort and challenge Cerys's contribution. I had noticed that Cerys was unaware of their discomfort. What I did was *'wonder aloud'* about how the children might be feeling, offering them a safe space in which to reflect upon and express their feelings.

All the children benefitted from this experience, because witnessing is another form of learning. Many children with Autism Spectrum Disorder or Asperger's Syndrome can get 'stuck' and hold grudges against someone else who has said or done something to hurt them in the past, because the uncertainty of what might happen if they let go of the grudges can be too overwhelming. The children in the Friendly Group repeatedly have experiences of feeling hurt *and* opportunities for learning what it feels like to let go of a grudge or a felt hurt. They learn how to say what they are feeling and to discover it is safe to do so, which helps to loosen their rigid thinking.

Reflective leadership

As I have already said in this chapter, the adult, while having a particular role of authority in the group, is nevertheless a group member too and will pick up the agitation and turbulent feelings just as the other group members do. Leadership is not only having the capacity to experience the turbulence and feel the feelings but also having the ability to stand back, think, explore and explain what is happening in ways that communicates to the group the heart of the matter. This is a crucial role in reflective group leadership; the ability to allow one's feelings to be stirred whilst still being able to make sense of what is happening and using this insight to help the children in the group develop the skills of *pause and reflection* within themselves. This is why it is so important that the group leader and colleagues properly process their own feelings and reflections after sessions through debriefing, professional supervision, and personal reflective notes.

> **THINGS TO THINK ABOUT**
>
> In this chapter we've seen how children can act out their uncertainties through rivalry between each other or in challenging adult authority. What I have described here happens in all groups. There will always be times when there are tensions, but if we understand better what is going on it helps us to 'step back' and see the dynamics for what they are, rather than becoming emotionally involved and feeling out of control ourselves. This is the case when running a group or family household.

CHAPTER 9

The Worry Bear and sensory issues

Sitting on one of the window sills in the group room is a small teddy bear. Well, he isn't technically sitting on the window sill, he's actually sitting on a little doll's size chair that reminds me of the one in the famous painting by Van Gogh. He is quite small, about 10 to 15 centimetres tall, and has moveable limbs. He is made out of white cotton fabric patterned with tiny blue flowers and has a blue ribbon around his neck. He is called the *Worry Bear.* The children have the opportunity to pick him up and talk about their worries. All children I have worked with have liked this bear and have been happy to handle it. However, once when I told a group of parents about how their children had been using the bear, a parent said,

> *"Well I bet Adrian has never picked the bear up and spoken about his worries!"* I replied that he had.
> *"Well I am very surprised,"* replied the parent, *"Adrian can't bear the feeling of the furry fabric of soft toys. He is funny about touching or wearing lots of different types of fabrics because of his sensory difficulties."*
> *"My child is just the same,"* interjected another, *"I even have to buy special clothes without seams and only of soft cotton."*
> *"The Worry Bear is made out of cotton,"* I explained.
> *"Then I guess he wouldn't mind picking it up and holding it!"* commented Adrian's mother.

Sensory issues

It's worth thinking carefully about the resources that we use in a group and ask children if it's okay for them to handle them. If the little bear had been made from a different type of fabric, like pretend fur, the children in this story may not have been able to share their worries. Not because they didn't want to but because they might have been too worried about having to touch the furry fabric.

I am mindful that children can feel overwhelmed by sensory overload and are then unable to manage the stress this creates. In the Friendly Group we have done ordinary things like closing the curtains because of bright sunlight, shutting the windows because of the draft or opening them because of stuffiness. However, there have been other times when we have had to quieten piano playing or laughter because of the loud noises, place a cloth on the floor because of the scratchy texture of the carpet, rearrange the seating because of the proximity of other children, remove a toy because it is too scary and various other accommodations. Whenever there are sensory issues, it becomes an opportunity to talk about worries, uncomfortable feelings and things the children do not like.

JEREMY'S WORRY ABOUT CAMPING

> *"This is the Worry Bear,"* announced Lee, (11) as he picked it off the little chair on the window sill, *"What you do is hold him and you tell him your worries and then you feel better."*
> *"Can I speak with the Worry Bear first?"* asked Jeremy (13).

For the first two years of attending the group, Jeremy had been unable to talk about himself or his feelings. He preferred to communicate about himself through the objects he brought to show the other children. When others talked about their feelings he would sit up stiffly and awkwardly, blushing if attention was ever drawn to him. In recent months I had noticed a change. As Jeremy massaged the bear between his fingers he began to talk.

> *"I have got lots of big worries at the moment. There are so many new things. I've started a new school; it's very nice there but it's difficult getting used to new things. And we have got to go camping with the school soon. It's for three nights and I've only been camping once. It was only for one night and it was a disaster. And I have never slept anywhere without my mum being there and the parents are not allowed to come and I'm not even allowed to take my phone. And I don't know how to put up a tent. We have to put up our own tents! And we have to cook our own breakfast, dinner and tea. It may not sound a big worry but it is for me."*

The words tumbled out without a pause. The children listened with intent interest.

> *"I go camping every year with my family and I love it!"* began Zoe, (12) *"But I can understand you might be worried if it is away from your family."*
> *"Yes! And I'm going away without any of my old friends. That's the worry. I don't really know the other people in my school yet,"* continued Jeremy.
> *"You could see it as a positive,"* added Zoe, *"This could be a time when you get to know your new friends a lot better."* *"I agree,"* said Marek.
> *"I know how you feel, Jeremy,"* added Nathaniel.
> *"You can ask someone who knows how to put up a tent, to help you,"* suggested Jaye. *"If they have been in the school for a while, they will have done this before and know what to do."*

"*Yes! It's always good to ask for help,*" said Trevor. Jeremy began to breathe more slowly and deeply and carefully placed the *Worry Bear* back in the middle of the circle. He then thanked everyone for listening and said that he felt better already. Jaye (13) then leant forward and picked up the bear.

> "*You've reminded me of something I'm worried about,*" said Jaye, leaning her back against the wall, "*I'm going on a school camping trip as well. The teacher is mixing up the groups so we're not with our friends. I know you don't know how to put up a tent Jeremy, but I* **do** *know, but no-one listens to me. I'm one of the weirdos at school, so no-one listens to me and it makes me really angry. If they are on their own with me they are nice, but if they're with their friends they want to be 'cool', so they only listen to the group and not to 'freaks' like me. Then I'm seen as 'super weird'. I hate them! Well I don't hate them, but I do hate their behaviour.*"

Jaye became quite agitated as she told her story. I could hear the family's use of language, which Jaye was echoing, like '*hating their behaviour*'. While most teenagers have their own lively way of speaking, many children on the autism spectrum mimic the language of adults. This often makes them stand out among their peers and seem different. On this day, you could have heard a pin drop. The attentive silence said it all; the children could recognise themselves in Jaye's story and accepted her use of language. She returned the bear to the circle and seemed calm, telling the others she felt better. She had found a group where she *was* listened to. She didn't want advice, she simply wanted to he heard.

Nathaniel (12) was the next to request the bear. Nathaniel had been a member of the Friendly Group for two years and had until recently, like Jeremy, been unable to talk about his feelings.

> "Jason was my best friend at my old school," said Nathaniel with an intent expression on his face. "Now he's not friends with me anymore. He's made new friends. I've said and done everything I can to make things better, but Jason throws it back in my face. I say to him that we used to be best friends and he says, 'Yes! We **used** to be'. I'm really worried that Jason won't be friends with me again. It has made me cry. I don't know what to do. I've tried everything."

With that, Nathaniel lowered his head and looked at the floor, his mop of dark curly hair hiding the sprouting tears, but his shrunken posture vividly betrayed his suffering. The atmosphere in the room changed; all the children looked in Nathaniel's direction and there was a charged silence because his story had touched them. It was their story too.

> "He'll come back and be friends sooner or later," said Jeremy.
> "People who haven't known Jason long are crowding him with friendship. They always gather round the new person," added Zoe. "When that calms down, he'll want to be friends with you again."
> "I agree with Zoe," said Jaye, "If he is a real friend, he'll come back. If he doesn't then he isn't a true friend anymore."
> "Just take it step by step. Small things like saying 'hello'," advised Zoe.
> "He doesn't say hello to me," whimpered Nathaniel.
> "Well, try to speak to him on his own," added Trevor, "In front of the others he may want to stay popular."
> "Last term I felt jealous of Jason's new friends. I felt hurt and left out," said Nathaniel in a stronger voice.

> *"Now it's the weekend, I would suggest that you try to push it from your mind,"* suggested Zoe.
>
> *"Yes!"* agreed Marek, *"You don't want to let it to spoil your weekend."*

Jeremy then offered his own personal story, which he hoped would bring Nathaniel a ray of hope.

> *"I had lots of friends at my old school till this 'cool guy' came to the school. All my friends went running to be with him and I was left out. Then he left the school and my friends all came back to me."*

The next week Nathaniel asked if he could speak first with the *Worry Bear*.

> *"I want to talk about Jason again,"* said Nathaniel as he looked round to see if everyone was listening.
>
> *"I'm really worried about Jason. He says it will take a long time for him to forgive me. But I have given him three weeks already. I'm worried because he says that maybe it will take a year and that is a really long time. I want to be friends with Jason again now."*
>
> *"I wonder what Jason thinks he has to forgive you for?"* I asked.
>
> *"It was in a triple games lesson that lasts two hours,"* explained Nathaniel, *"We were going to the hockey pitch and I said I hated Jason. I didn't really mean it but I just needed some time alone. Jason didn't understand. Now he says he won't forgive me for saying that."*

It was at this point that I felt I needed to say something. The rest of the children were completely quiet. They did not know what to say. There was an atmosphere of helplessness and hopelessness. I then asked the group if anyone of them had ever said something mean or hateful to someone they cared about. I put my hand up first. One by one everyone else had put their hands up. Nathaniel glanced at the sea of raised hands.

> *"We all say things that we regret,"* I said.
> *"Perhaps he doesn't mean he won't be friends for a year. I'm sure he will come back,"* added Marek.
> *"He might have some other friends. Does your friend Jason have other friends, Nathaniel?"* asked Jeremy. *"Yes, he does,"* answered Nathaniel.
> *"Do you like any of his friends?"* Jeremy continued: Nathaniel said he did.
> *"Well why don't you ask those friends you do like to join in their game? Then you will be playing near Jason,"* suggested Jeremy.
> *"I've tried that,"* said Nathaniel, *"and I did get to play with Jason's friends but Jason didn't talk to me. He just ignored me."*

Zoe then asked how long ago was it that the comment on the way to the hockey pitch happened and we were all surprised to hear that it was in the winter term; about five or six months earlier.

> *"Well, I think that Jason doesn't deserve to have your friendship,"* said Jaye, looking straight at Nathaniel. *"You are a really nice person and if he was a true friend he would have forgiven you by now. I suggest you try to find some other friends."*
> *"Don't worry Nathaniel, it will all be OK,"* said Marek as he put his arm round Nathaniel's shoulder.
> *"Thank you! I guess you are right!"*

The discussion in this group, over a two week period, brought up preoccupations that all the children feel at some time or another, particularly during puberty and adolescence: that of wanting friends but feeling rejected and isolated. The children's comments reflected their own feelings about themselves. Those who are eager to offer advice, solutions or say that everything will be okay, do so to make themselves feel better, as it is unbearable to think about their own difficulties. Those who hold grudges against others because of their own experiences of rejection reflect back their own 'stuck' positions by encouraging rejection as a way forward.

However, the very fact that the group was listening to Nathaniel and Jeremy and taking their worries seriously helped them both. They were able to think and talk about what was troubling them. This helped them to process what was happening in their lives. They felt less isolated and it gave them a clearer picture about how to move forward. The adults supported the discussion by 'holding the space' and allowing the whole group to share their thoughts and feelings without interruption.

Jeremy had a successful camping trip and was able to not only share his positive experience, but also expressed his appreciation for the group's support. He went on to have a happy time in this new school. Nathaniel began to join in with Jason's group and felt less upset and frustrated by Jason's rejection. I was to learn that Jason too was on the autism spectrum and struggled with relationships because of his rigid thinking and tendency towards holding grudges. The boys were never able to renew their friendship, but Nathaniel became more understanding of Jason's behaviour over the course of the next year and was able to let the upset pass.

THINGS TO THINK ABOUT

When children or young people have a safe space to share their worries it is very empowering. The very act of saying aloud your worries helps you to see them in a more detached way so you feel calmer and a way forward becomes clearer. What the children discovered in this story was that they were not alone in their worries and that others had had similar experiences. They were genuinely able to help each other. The group leaders listened and participated, not by adding advice, views or guiding the discussion. We were there offering these children unspoken permission to speak openly, with them knowing that we would intervene if necessary.

In this chapter I have illustrated how a simple resource, the *Worry Bear*, can be used to help children share their worries. When children are able to open up in this way together, it deepens their relationships. In the next chapter I'll tell some stories about how two outdoor resources have helped children to deepen their relationships through supporting each other in their play.

CHAPTER 10

The trolley and the trampoline

The trolley

One afternoon, some years before I set up the Friendly Group, my daughter, 11 at the time, came out of school with her friend to walk home as usual. What wasn't usual was that there was a skip outside the school gate full of rubbish. The two girls noticed that there was a trolley in the skip and decided it would be fun to retrieve this object, put their rucksacks on board and pull it home. As our house was the first port of call (about a mile from school), and my daughter's friend still had another half a mile to go, the trolley was abandoned at our house. It was then put in the garden shed and largely forgotten. It was only much later I realised what this trolley was for and where it came from. The school is opposite a small hospital and the trolley was probably used by porters to transport heavy boxes and the like from one part of the hospital to the other. It seemed an ideal outdoor resource to take to the Friendly Group.

MARLON'S STORY

Marlon came to one of my very first groups. He was a nervous boy and found it difficult to get on with the other children. In the circle, he brought objects to show the others rather than talk about his experiences. When we talked about feelings Marlon often cried or got angry. He was eight, and a tall stocky boy for his age. He had a mop of thick curly black hair and wore large old-fashioned glasses which exaggerated his moon shaped face.

During the *choosing time* part of the session Marlon would tend to play on his own with the wooden bricks or line up the plastic dinosaurs. But he was clumsy and when they fell over this frustrated him, and he would abandon the play. He didn't know how to engage with the other children. When he was outside he just stood awkwardly, gazing into the middle distance. Then he discovered the trolley. He simply pulled it round the garden area, and the handle and wheels responded to his touch. Many of the children walk or run in the open space, some walk round the boundary or, if braver, explore the hidden paths and play chasing games on the grass. Marlon liked to have something in his hands. The trolley gave him something to hold and a means to move around the space. If a child asked for a ride, he let them clamber on. He didn't have to talk but he was having the experience of doing something *with* someone else. His confidence quickly grew and he liked to be seen as the person who gave rides. Marlon's size meant he had the strength to pull children fast even over the bumpiest parts of the garden, and they were soon 'queuing up' for a ride.

It was not long before he was the first outside at choosing time to claim the trolley and call out *"Anyone for a ride?"* This play developed over some weeks and became more elaborate as Marlon created 'stations', where children could board or disembark. He named parts of the garden area as different 'worlds' that the children could visit; the stinky swamp, the fairy glen, the dark jungle, to name but a few. He then cut up some pieces of paper and offered tickets for the rides. The final element came when he discovered a cap (in the box of hats) that resembled a station master's cap. Through playing with the trolley, Marlon had found a safe way to connect with the other children; he had created a role for himself.

OSCAR'S STORY

In another group, there was Oscar. He was a rather different boy. At home he often had emotional meltdowns and couldn't stop screaming. One of the things he couldn't cope with were family gatherings when there was a lot of laughter. To calm down he would have to withdraw to his own special room in the house. He also screamed when he had to leave the house to get on the school taxi. He screamed when he got back to his house at the end of the day. The transition from the quiet of home to the noise and bustle in the shared taxi was too much for him. Oscar couldn't regulate the tensions that had built up during the day and he let them off the minute he got home. A raised voice or an unexpected movement triggered Oscar's anxiety and he could become silent, frozen on the spot. He was nine. His parents wondered if he would cope with the Friendly Group.

At the beginning Oscar was very quiet and compliant, but he seemed to enjoy the predictable structure of the group. His parents were relieved because he wanted to come and there were no meltdowns at home. In the *Circle Time* part of the session he usually said, *"I have nothing to say right now,"* when it was his turn with the stone, but I noticed that he seemed to listen with interest to the others' contributions. I noticed, too, that while Oscar presented as an incredibly timid boy, in the stories the group created he often introduced monsters or obstacles, which he would bravely overcome.

This gave me a clue. Oscar wanted excitement and courage but was too timid to step over the line. When we went outside I could see his fascination with the trolley but also the way his body tensed up in terror if there were any suggestion he might like to go on it.

> *"Would you like a ride on the trolley?"* offered Calum, who was older and a more established member of the group.
> *"No thank you,"* whispered Oscar as he walked swiftly away to avoid being pressed into something as terrifying as sitting on that fast moving rubbery board.

> *"I think that Oscar might be worried that you will pull the trolley too fast,"* I commented in Calum's earshot.
> *"I will go slowly Oscar!"* said Calum, as he hurried in Oscar's direction. Oscar froze and ignored Calum.
> *"Calum, that is a kind thing to offer, but Oscar is a bit too nervous to try the trolley just yet. That's OK. Go and see if someone else would like a ride and Oscar can watch,"* I interjected to Calum, ensuring that Oscar could also hear me.

Calum found another child and the two of them took turns with the trolley. The trolley bashed against the wall and I could see Oscar wince, but I also noticed a little smile creep over his face as he saw the trolley whiz along.

> *"It's scary to imagine letting someone pull you,"* I commented to Oscar in a way that meant he didn't have to answer me. *"You don't know if they will stop when you want them to or if they will go slowly enough."*
> Oscar nodded.
> *"Maybe you would like to pull the trolley yourself sometime?"* I continued. Oscar didn't move except to look down at the ground. I'd gone one step too far and too fast, realised what I'd said and added, *"It's OK! You don't have to go on it or pull it at all unless you want to. In the Friendly Group no-one makes you do anything that feels uncomfortable."*

Oscar relaxed and when we talked again in the circle at the end of the session, I was able to reflect with the whole group about how the children use the trolley and how it can be both exciting and scary. Over the next few sessions, there were interesting developments. Oscar continued to watch other children use the trolley. He was beginning to relax as he trusted he wouldn't be forced to join in. Then one day, the trolley was left unused for a while. Oscar walked up to it and looked round to check if anyone was near.

> *"It's OK,"* I said, *"If you want to touch the trolley, I'll make sure that no-one else will try and use it."*

My timing was better on this occasion, because Oscar went up to it and picked up the long handle. He pulled it along the path a few feet then successfully brought it to a controlled stop. He then bent forward and gently stroked the fine rubbery ribs of the board and felt the trolley move a little.

> *"It moves very easily, doesn't it Oscar?"* I added, *"If I hold it steady, would you like to try sitting on it? I shall make sure that it won't move."*

Oscar looked at me and whispered an assent as I crouched down to be at his sitting height, holding the trolley frame steady. Oscar lowered himself down, with his feet straddling either side and gripping the rim. He began to smile.

> *"Would you like me to pull you as far as the table?"* I offered. The table was only a few feet away.

Oscar continued to smile as we rolled the few feet and came to a stop. At that moment a couple of other children appeared and Oscar immediately got off.

> *"I wonder if you two would be prepared to hold the handle and let Oscar just sit on the trolley without it moving,"* I suggested.

The two children, a boy and girl, did exactly that, and more.

"It's okay, Oscar," said Evie in a reassuring voice. "We'll show you. Gwyn, can you sit on the trolley and I'll just hold the handle to show Oscar how we can keep it steady?"

Gwyn sat on the immobile trolley and looked at Oscar. "I used to be scared like you. But it's okay, we promise we won't move unless you ask us."

In that extraordinary moment, there was every element of a friendship being played out. Gwyn and Evie were tuning in to Oscar's feelings. They could sense his lack of trust and wanted to reassure him. They respected his wish to sit still. Gwyn acknowledged his feelings, was empathic and showed he understood how Oscar felt, even adding that he too had been afraid. Evie was offering that she and Gwyn could demonstrate how they would hold the trolley for Oscar, monitoring their behaviour to build up trust. And almost the most important thing of all was that they were giving unconditional acceptance. What a true act of kindness.

Oscar then climbed on the trolley and Gwyn and Evie held the handle. Slowly but surely they talked Oscar into being pulled very gently until he was being pulled at quite a good speed along the grass. Oscar even giggled loudly as he held on and other children ran beside them. There was a group thrill that Oscar was on the trolley.

As the weeks went by Oscar became braver, went faster and also began to find his voice and trust that children would stop when he asked them to. He now gave other children rides too. The trolley was his favourite bit of the session at that time. There was, however, one final taboo. The most exciting trick that the children had learned was to pull the trolley down the three stone steps from the grass to the paved area. Although the steps are shallow and the transit is perfectly safe, it gives a rather thrilling experience to bump down them. Adults are always observant to ensure the children are safe. However, Oscar made it quite clear he would not try that trick!

Nevertheless he became excited simply watching and would be within range every time this was going on. It was as if he was inwardly imagining and rehearsing what the experience would be like. He wanted the thrill for himself, but it was just a step too far to take the risk and do it for real. Until one day he did. A few small steps; but with those steps Oscar discovered a new confidence in himself and basked in the shared delight of his friends. Needless to say this play was repeated over and over and was enjoyed till the day he left the group some years later.

Bringing children together

So how else has the trolley brought children together? Sometimes there have been as many as five children playing together as three have squeezed on the tight space and been pulled by two others. At other times soft toys have been given rides or bulky play equipment has been transported from one place to another. During one summer holiday group (when the children spend a week together), they collaborated to create a car. They found a large box which they fixed to the trolley, then made four wheels from pizza bases and stuck them on the side. They cut out a steering wheel and a windscreen for the front, and finally a number plate was added. At the end of the sessions, the children agreed to dismantle the car so we could have the original trolley back.

The trampoline

From the beginning of March till the beginning of November, there is a large (8 foot diameter) outdoor trampoline that the children can use. It is a wonderful resource for individual children, but has extra value in the group, when the children can have experiences of playing with another and taking turns in a non-threatening way.

It interests me how children can immediately relax on the trampoline as they regulate the pleasurable experiences of bounce with the safety of feeling in control.

The sensations of touch and flight, rhythm and spaciousness together with feelings of containment within the circular mat all seem to release some of their initial anxiety and tensions.

MIRIAM'S FIRST VISIT

There was a knock on the door and when I opened it I was greeted by Miriam's mother wearing a dismayed expression. *"She won't get out of the car,"* she said in a desperate tone of voice.

The car was parked on the road immediately outside the entrance. I could hear a car door shut and then saw a movement. A small girl ran silently in through the driveway entrance and immediately hid behind a wall leading to the garden. This was my first encounter with Miriam (10).

I used the tactic of talking to her mother quite loudly so that Miriam could hear. This is something we often do intuitively with very young children who are nervous of strangers. It is a way of passing information through the mother's ear to the child's. The mother is still there for protection and acts as a monitor for what is alright to hear and respond to. The mother becomes a safe filter. The fact that I was keeping the dialogue as a threesome was helping the mother with this transition too.

> *"I'm so pleased you have brought Miriam today. It is sunny and warm and when she is ready she can have a bounce on the trampoline if she likes,"* I said.

I knew from her mother that Miriam loved trampolines and didn't have one herself. I was giving Miriam the opportunity to make a safe entrance. I had invited her to come in when she was ready. What I was doing was allowing her to take control of the timing and I had also suggested something she could specifically do. This would take away some of the 'anxiety provoking uncertainty' for her.

Miriam peeped out from behind the wall and made a dash towards a shrub that was nearer to the trampoline. Although she was more visible now, I did not make eye contact with her. This could have felt too overwhelming for her. Instead, I let her know I was still thinking about her, by talking to her mother. *"Let's go and check that the trampoline is dry for Miriam,"* I continued and the two of us walked towards it.

Miriam then ran to the trampoline herself, and paused. She seemed unsure about climbing up on the mat. She seemed to mutter to herself, rather than speaking directly to me or her mother. *"There's no net …"*

In recent years I have had several comments from the children that the trampoline doesn't look safe because it has no net. In some way, the children are not only expressing a concern about their physical safety but they are also checking out their emotional safety. What will this woman say? Will she listen to me? Will she keep me safe?

"I can understand you might be a bit worried to see a trampoline without a net," I usually say, thus naming and acknowledging the child's feelings. I ask whether the child has one at home, showing an interest in the child and giving her a chance to talk about her experiences of trampolines. Most children have usually jumped on one even if they don't have one at home. If a child has a trampoline I ask whether they have a net, how big their trampoline is and where it is located in their garden. Some children tell me even without the prompting questions. I invite them to tell me what they think the net is for and why they like the net. These are the usual kinds of comments the children make.

> *"The net keeps you safe and you don't fall off."*
> *"I like playing with my ball on the trampoline and it bounces off the net."*
> *"Mummy thinks the net keeps you safe."*

> So I say, *"Those are good reasons. Shall I tell you why this trampoline has no net?" "Yes please!"* is the usual reply.
> *"Well when there is no net you have to **pay attention**. You have to **think** about what you are doing. You are perfectly safe if you jump in the middle. When you are thinking about what you are doing you take care of yourself and keep yourself safe. And I and the others will be watching you. There will always be a grown-up here to watch you. Have a go if you like!"* I explain.

The child takes off their shoes (at my request) and climbs onto the black mat. Some children show great competence and jump high, do sit jumps, star jumps and even flips. Others simply bend their knees a bit causing a gentle movement, without actually taking flight at all. I make positive comments about their experience (rather than their skills) and then begin to tell them how the trampoline is used in the group.

I had this very kind of conversation with Miriam and she carefully unlaced her bright pink trainers before clambering up. I continued.

> *"In the Friendly Group, I allow up to three children at a time on the trampoline. But if you want to use it on your own, you can. A grown-up will be with you all the time. There are three other rules; no food, no touching of other people and no hard objects."*

Children like clear rules. It makes them feel safe. I also go on to explain about the reasons why there may be such rules. If the child is quite chatty I invite him or her to give their ideas about what those reasons might be. Miriam was by now bouncing gently on the trampoline and, like so many children, beginning to talk.

> *"Well, you wouldn't want crumbs on the trampoline,"* she began, *"And if you do play fighting on the trampoline, I guess someone could get hurt or fall off."*
> *"I agree,"* was my reply, *"And if you had a hard object in your hand it could cut the trampoline mat or accidentally hurt someone jumping next to you."*

For the more reticent children, who, unlike Miriam, stand stiffly at the edge, mute and unable to make that first move, I might talk about something impersonal such as the structure of the trampoline and its new springs. I invite the child to try it out and give me their view on the bounciness and how it compares with other trampolines they might have tried. The conversation is kept safely neutral, but I am inviting them to share something of themselves by asking their opinion. When they start talking, whether it is about the trampoline or something more personal about themselves, I reflect back what they say. Something like, *"Oh! So you've got a trampoline"* or *"I can hear you like playing with Lego."* In this way, they both hear what they've said and know that I've listened. In addition I 'wonder aloud' about how these things make them feel. For example, a boy (on his first visit) recently told me about a forthcoming house move (another uncertainty) he was facing.

> *"I wonder how that feels for you? Some children find the idea of moving house exciting, but others are worried about the change. I don't know what it's like for you,"* I said.

I wasn't asking a direct question. However, I was giving him the opportunity to be drawn into a two-way conversation by showing interest, not making assumptions and inviting some reflection. When I do this, the response varies from curt and factual comments to long and involved monologues, but this kind of introduction usually helps children to settle and feel more confident.

After about five minutes or so on the trampoline, Miriam was ready to come inside to find out more about the group. Her mother had witnessed how the trampoline had mediated the transition from leaving the familiar safety of the family car to meeting and talking to a stranger.

Togetherness on a trampoline

What I've noticed about the trampoline is that however quiet a child might be, once they start jumping they start talking! What's more, they often spontaneously start talking about their feelings. I usually discover more about a child's life and his hopes and fears in the few minutes on the trampoline than at any other time.

The trampoline also seems to facilitate ease between children, enabling them to feel comfortable in the company of each other. So how does the trampoline help children towards building relationships? Have you ever been on a trampoline with someone else? The surface is unsteady enough as it is when you jump alone but when someone else is jumping then you lose control and find yourself wobbling, falling, or being thrown high into the air. And do you know what, it makes you laugh! In all the years that I have worked with children, it's the first thing I notice when more than one of them tries to jump together. They can't help smiling. The smiles then irresistibly turn into giggles and then often become whoops of laughter. The spontaneous laughter of children is a joyful gift for anyone.

Release from control enables growth and learning

The trampoline offers a new kind of experience for children who tend towards control as a way of managing anxiety. Once a child can feel that the trampoline structure is safe and the adults nearby are relaxed about them bouncing, they can begin to experiment with what they can do with their bodies on it. There are such pleasures in bouncing; it's about learning a different rhythm and about letting go. There is a release from the rigid 'holding on' as a child regulates the control and release for themselves. They discover they can feel safe and have fun at the same time. They begin to have a physical experience of regulating and releasing anxiety, and this means a lot at a psychological level. They're learning, in a safe way, about taking risks, coming out of their comfort zone and how to be playful.

Both parents and children alike, who are lucky enough to have regular access to a trampoline, say how helpful it is to have a 'good bounce' after a stressful day at school.

BRENDAN AND KAYLEIGH'S STORY

Brendan (9) was extremely anxious when he started the Friendly Group. He couldn't bear uncertainty and wanted to control everything in his life from the particular breakfast cereal he would eat to the elaborate bedtime rituals. The group was well outside his comfort zone and his anxiety manifested in his body as a fixed grin on his face and incredibly tight neck muscles. Any attempt on my part to alleviate his anxiety by explaining what was happening or going to happen during those early sessions, was met with *"I know that, Anita. You don't have to tell me!"*

On the visit before meeting the group, Brendan had delighted in jumping on the trampoline on his own, but when he started the group he insisted that he would *only* go on the trampoline on his own. He didn't want to jump with other children. That was fine, but he had to find a way to ask the other children for this arrangement. Brendan stood at the edge of the trampoline watching three children bouncing together. He began to turn away and was about to give up.

"In the Friendly Group, we are kind to one another," I reminded the jumping trio. *"This means noticing what someone else wants and offering to help. I wonder how you can be kind to Brendan when you can see he might like a go."*

Brendan turned back, curious to see what would happen next.

> *"I'll get off if you like,"* volunteered one of the jumpers as he moved towards the edge.
> *"No thank you!"* said Brendan, in what sounded like a rather sharp tone.
> *"Brendan has told me that he would prefer to jump on his own,"* I added, so that all of the jumpers could hear. I knew that on this occasion Brendan would not be able to find those words for himself.
> *"Here you go!"* said each of the jumpers as they clambered off the trampoline. The mat was now empty.
> *"I wonder what you could say, Brendan?"* I asked as he stood there, mute.
> *"Thank you,"* said Brendan.

The others briefly smiled, but moments later abandoned Brendan and the trampoline. Their social skills did not extend to talking to Brendan or imagining that he might simply like some company. Meanwhile Brendan climbed on and began to jump and talk to me. He was more comfortable talking with adults and, as an only child, had learnt the skills of charming adult relatives and teachers. They were more predicable in their responses than his own peer group, whom he largely avoided.

It was not long before another child approached the trampoline. Kayleigh (11) was wearing her winter coat with the hood up even though the weather was getting warmer. It was like her protective shell. She simply stood at the edge of the trampoline, head slightly bowed to avoid eye contact. Brendan chose to ignore her and she said nothing. Once again, I stepped in with a comment.

> *"It looks like Kayleigh wants a go on the trampoline. I wonder what we can do?"*

Both the children continued as they were, so I had to be more direct and asked Kayleigh if she would like a go and she said she would, to me, but not to Brendan. So I invited her to ask Brendan herself. Brendan was fully aware of the whole exchange.

> *"Can I have a go?"* asked Kayleigh in barely a whisper.
> *"Okay, then I'll get off,"* replied Brendan.
> I could see that Brendan was simply going to withdraw from the situation. This was when I stepped in again.
> *"You don't actually have to get off Brendan, as you know that up to three can be on the trampoline at the same time. If you like you could sit on the green padded edge, while Kayleigh has a go,"* I suggested.
> It was at this point that Kayleigh herself stepped in and said, *"It's okay, Brendan, I won't jump high."*

So Brendan tentatively sat on the edge, clinging on to the outer frame while Kayleigh jumped up and down. Kayleigh seemed to relax and soon she even shed her coat! But Brendan looked uncomfortable and also a bit stuck. I guessed he didn't want to actually get off until Kayleigh had stopped jumping and all was still. So I gently intervened once again.

> *"I wonder if Brendan would like to try jumping with Kayleigh sitting on the edge,"* I ventured, pausing to allow time for this idea to be processed by both of them. *"Of course Kayleigh would have to stop jumping to let Brendan have a go."*

In that moment a rather magical thing happened. Two children who found it so very difficult to navigate delicate social situations made a connection. Kayleigh stopped jumping and invited Brendan to have his go. She said that she could sit on the edge or get off altogether, but Brendan said she didn't have to do that; he would try jumping with her if she sat on the mat. In moments smiles crept across Kayleigh's face as Brendan's leaps sent her all over the mat. Brendan's whole demeanour changed; there was less tension in his body. I wondered if it was because he was loosening his need to control. In a gloriously unselfconscious and spontaneous few minutes the two of them ignored me and experimented with taking turns at sitting and jumping. They had been playing together. They had begun to trust one another.

At the end of the session, when we all sat in the circle together, I invited the children to reflect on moments of kindness. When it came to Kayleigh's turn, this is what she had to say.

> *"I was kind to Brendan because I let him have a go on the trampoline."*
> Kayleigh then glanced at Brendan, who smiled. *"I know that he normally wants to go on it by himself but he let me go on with him today and we had a lot of fun together. I think I was kind because he wasn't scared."*

Kayleigh had never spoken in this way before and she became rather red-faced in the process. However the brief exchange of smiles between Kayleigh and Brendan, as she reflected on what had happened further reinforced the connection the two of them had made.

THINGS TO THINK ABOUT

I remember what Neil Armstrong famously said, on stepping on the moon's surface, *"That's one small step for (a) man, one giant leap for mankind."* And I think about the hundreds of children I have worked with over the years. Sometimes it is the smallest of exchanges or steps forward that pave the way for the biggest changes and leaps forward in children's development. I am so grateful to all the children like Marlon, Oscar, Kayleigh and Brendan who have taught me the importance of 'small is beautiful,' and that we need to be patient with and attentive towards all children, particularly those who are anxious and sensitive.

Imagination: the story and the obstacle course

All children use narrative or pretend play in order to express their imagination. It's a human capacity that is expressed, explored and developed throughout life. Being able to imagine oneself as another person or in another person's place is important for developing the skills in making social relationships. It also allows an experience of being 'invited in' to the imaginal world; finding one's own sense of self, that inner core, the unchanging aspect of ourselves from where we can explore and venture into the new. Imagination is creative, giving form to new images and sensations that are not perceived directly through one's sight, hearing or the other senses. One form of expressing imagination is through the medium of stories, and making up stories is at the core of the Friendly Group session.

With limited imagination we can't make links, and life just becomes a series of episodes that don't connect. However, through imagination, the mind creates a network of connections; it is the great linking capacity. The stories we tell about our lives allow us to create our social and personal history. *"Can you remember when we ... ?"* deepens relationships and a sense of connectedness as one's past history is brought into the present and more links are made. Memories are about recreating our own life stories.

Imagination allows you to take yourself beyond the realm of practical possibility and yet have a direct emotional and sensational experience. It's exciting and playful to use one's imagination. Imagination is a kind of fantasy and acts as a bridge between the conscious and the unconscious mind. However this kind of fantasy shouldn't be confused with the inner world of the fantasist who makes up stories and believes they are true. The fantasy world of that kind is a defence structure that takes the person outside the pain and confusion of everyday life. I have met children over the years, who have told untrue stories about themselves and have either been in denial about their falseness or who have been puzzled over why they told them. These fantasies have brought them no pleasure and are an indication that they need help and support rather than be chastised for telling untruths.

When the children and young people make up their stories in the Friendly Group, they recognise it to be 'pretend' and can be very playful and creative with it. Even those children who are very literal thinkers can still take part in this activity and be playful. It is important to recognise that play is a deep form of communication.

What shall we take?

When *creating a story* together in the group (*as described in* Chapter 4) the children are often invited to imagine two or three objects that they might like to take with them on their story quest or journey. In one particular group of nine to eleven year olds, there were the two newcomers, Arlo and Vishal, and they were keen to be the first two to give their ideas about items to take. It was agreed that Arlo (11) would speak first, followed by Vishal (9). The rest of the group were happy with this. Here's an edited extract from their story as it was typed out and printed for the children. It was written in the present tense and the words used in the narrative are those used by the children.

```
"I want to take a gun that fires a million bullets a
minute," says Arlo, "and it would be a good idea to take
climbing equipment too. I also want to take a freeze
```

> *ray gun, scuba diving equipment and a ghost suit to walk through objects."*
> *"I think I would like to take a compass,"* says Vishal.
> *"I would like to take a helmet,"* says Andrew.
> *Toby says that he wants to take a fire staff, a fire proof suit and some harpoons and Lawrence suggests taking a missile shooter.*
> *"I want to take lots of food and drink,"* says Ram, *"lots of pizzas and sweets and hot chocolate."*
> *Lee decides to take intangibility gloves and night vision goggles.*
> *Rick tells us that he would like to take an infinite pack of C4 type of explosives and a Glock 18 gun.*

It is always interesting to examine what the children and young people choose. The children who are new to the group invariably choose weapons. Reading this as a metaphor, they might be expressing their uncertainty by carrying objects with which to defend themselves. In this case, Arlo is making sure that he has a gun that fires a million bullets a minute. He is taking no chances! His choices can also reveal other aspects of himself. We might imagine that climbing equipment suggests he wants to reach up and climb high; he might have a sense of ambition. Scuba diving equipment suggests he wants to go deep and maybe search more deeply within himself.

Rick, Toby and Lawrence also choose weapons; all three struggle with high levels of anxiety. Vishal, another new boy decides to take a compass. Is he trying to get his bearings? Andrew's choice of a helmet suggests his desire for protection and containment. Ram wants to take food, suggesting his desire to satisfy both his physical needs as well as his need for emotional and mental nourishment.

When children work with metaphor through *creating stories*, they are being given the space to use their imaginations to work through their preoccupations. The attentiveness of the adults is important, paying attention to the children's undigested experiences and habits of thinking. Some common themes include:

- Becoming a baddy
- Needing to be rescued
- Wanting food (nurture)
- Wanting to give others food
- Going through portals to other times and places
- Getting buried deep
- Squeezing through narrow places
- Killing or outwitting an enemy
- Getting separated from the others

Story themes and interpretation

Generally the stories the children create take the themes of a journey or a quest. These are two of the central storylines that have threaded through humanity from the earliest times to the present day. Familiar stories of journeys could include *Orpheus in the Underworld* and *Alice in Wonderland*, and quests could include the *Odyssey*, *Pilgrim's Progress* and *Watership Down,* let alone any number of films, TV programmes and games on these themes the children may or not be aware of. The words 'quest' and 'question' come from the same root and their definitions are both associated with a search for meaning. However, while a question engages the rational mind and requires conscious cognition, a quest in the form of a story engages the unconscious mind through the realm of imagination. When we enter the realm of imagination the self-conscious restrictions of judgemental and analytical thought evaporate, and one's inner truths can surface and be experienced, expressed and processed. Stories and storytelling provide a profoundly satisfying and invigorating pathway to finding meaning in our lives. We only need to remember the last time we read a good novel or watched a good film to know the truth that story enriches lives whatever age we are.

Although children are not consciously aware of the common structures of a story, they nevertheless tend to follow them. These are:

- Setting off on an adventure with feelings of anticipation
- Going to new and unfamiliar places - an island, a planet, under the earth, a forest
- Things are going well: there are some successes and discoveries and there is time to play and feast
- Things begin to go wrong; the vehicle is damaged, there are obstructions, they are confronted with an enemy or monster, there are temptations, they get lost, the group becomes separated but they still overcome all these difficulties
- Things begin to go very wrong, some kind of disaster erupts and it seems all hope is lost; often an individual takes the lead
- There is a resolution and the crisis is overcome. The group come together to reach their goal and then return home; this stage is often exciting with group collaboration and high risk.

What I have found very interesting is that in some groups the story has not got very far. We may still be at the setting-off stage and it is already week three. Indeed there have been some stories where the children have not gone anywhere at all. They have spent five weeks arguing over where to go and have never actually set off on a journey. In the early days of this type of work I found myself feeling frustrated, then realised that this reflected the dynamic of the group. Such groups have simply got stuck for the moment. It may be that the children are not yet feeling enough of a group; they are still a collection of separate individuals. As the children become more familiar with each other and trust each other then the story begins to develop and they get unstuck. Indeed the whole story is a metaphor for how the individuals in the group relate to each other. It raises all sorts of questions. Can they collaborate? Can they share? Can they empathise? Are these the qualities that bring about the resolution in the story?

Working with metaphor in this way also raises another very important issue; that of interpretation. Interpretation is about seeing meaning and going below the surface of what is being said so we can understand things better. Interpretation is asking questions, wondering about things and receiving the gifts of insight and other perspectives. Interpretation is never the 'answer'; it is simply a key to opening the issue further. What we see when we open the door and go through the doorway is always through our own personal lens. I receive communication from the children all the time, not only in the story part, but throughout the sessions in what they say, do or how they play and with what they play. However, as the adult, I need to be careful about offering interpretations.

When a child arms himself with weaponry for a journey story, I might simply say *"I can see that you need a lot of weapons to help you feel safe and strong for this journey."* A choice of weaponry is a communication to me about how they might need to arm themselves to face new situations, reflecting the insecurity or anxiety that the child might be feeling. There is then the question about what the source of anxiety or insecurity might be. The insecurity may reflect a child's position in the group. Is he new? Is he established but feels threatened by a newcomer? Does he want to assert his authority? There may also be a completely different reason. The child might be choosing to take a risk by experimenting with new facets of his personality, like being brave, strong or a leader. The weapons are a metaphor for the developing qualities in the child. While the children are playing on the surface, the adults look below the surface and help the children to look below the surface themselves.

However the first thing to do is to make sure that the child is properly listened to and heard; getting the right kind of attention. We can only begin to interpret metaphorical communication when we are on the particular wavelength of that child.

Can telling a story in a group be too difficult?

When a child tells a story he is able to create a narrative that has meaning for him. The child is able to link ideas and make connections. He is in charge of the story's direction and action, who the hero is, whether or not there are monsters or baddies, how scary it will be and whether it will have a resolution or not at the end.

When children tell a story in a group, they are creating a narrative that reflects both the group dynamic as well as their personal dynamic. They are exploring feelings about themselves as well as their feelings about others. They are experimenting with various aspects of themselves, like being brave or a leader (when they are normally timid) and how it feels to collaborate or to hurt within the safety of the story being only 'pretend'. The experience of taking part in creating a group story can be challenging for some children. The lack of 'personal control' in group storytelling can trigger overwhelming anxiety in some children. This happened to Lee.

LEE'S STORY

Lee (8) had told me he loved the 'idea' of the story part of the session when we met just before he started the group. However, on that first Saturday, he insisted on not only being the first to speak but also telling his own story in one 'go'. He only wanted his ideas. It was so overwhelming for him when another child began with other ideas, which could go in a different direction, that Lee began wailing and screaming. He stood up and took himself into the adjoining room. One of my colleagues joined him and, sitting at a table in quiet seclusion, he rapidly drew a series of cartoon type pictures recounting his story as he did so, while my colleague wrote down his words.

He calmed down instantly. At that time Lee was feeling separate and unconnected with the group. He was unable to see that what the others might say could be useful to him.

Meanwhile, in the main group room, the rest of the children had been unsettled by the commotion and waited anxiously for what would happen next.

> *"It's alright,"* I said to them, *"Lee has got such a lot of ideas that he finds it very difficult to listen to anyone else's at the moment. He is OK in the other room doing his part of the story and we can carry on with the main story here together."*

Acknowledging Lee's difficulty and saying that it was okay for him to be in another room calmed the group, and they were able to continue. This scenario was then repeated over the next few weeks. The children let Lee go first and he went in the other room, now more calmly (he always returned to the group when the story part was over). The following term, we started a new story and Lee was able to remain in the group room and tolerate hearing others' ideas, so long as he went first. The children tried to incorporate his ideas into their bits of the story. Lee, who had been so separate to begin with, became more curious about the group narrative and in turn began to relate more with the others. Then there came the week when one of the other children decided that he wanted to go first. The tension rose as Caleb and Lee faced each other from opposite sides of the circle, each insisting that they wanted to go first.

> *"I wonder if Lee knows how to be kind. He has had the first turn each week and knows that it gives him a good feeling. Maybe he would like to give the good feeling to Caleb and let him go first this week?"* I said in a slow steady voice.

I did not expect Lee to respond positively, but he did. He lowered his head in rather a submissive posture (avoiding any eye contact) and then nodded in Caleb's direction. This was his way of indicating that he would let Caleb go first. The spontaneous thanks expressed by Caleb seemed to break through some of Lee's autistic wall. He smiled briefly and I acknowledged for all of them that it was a big thing for Lee to do and I wondered how he was feeling.

> *"It's OK,"* he said, *"I still like going first but Caleb can go first this time. I want to go next,"* he added, making sure that he was second to speak!

In that moment he had managed to find a way of expressing disappointment, without wailing like a helpless infant might, and he had experienced a different and more expansive way of being. I was not sure whether his response was triggered by anxiety or whether he was expressing the more developed and positive feeling of concern. It didn't matter because my invitation and his response allowed him to behave 'as if' he cared about Caleb's response. Whatever his motivation on that day, it was the beginning of Lee's developing capacity for empathy and concern for others and was a huge step towards his social integration.

The obstacle course as metaphor

Children can express their imagination in many ways. Several years ago, at the end of a penultimate session for the term in a mixed group of teenagers, Zac (14) asked, *"Can we do something creative next week?"* I agreed and offered to bring in some empty cardboard boxes of various sizes, together with parcel tape, string and scissors. The session started in the usual way. However, I wasn't prepared for what happened next!

> *"Can we do something with those boxes now?"* requested Seth (15).

"Of course you can!" I replied, curious to see what they would do.

"Let's take them outside," suggested Graham, who always enjoyed making things.

The comfortable and familiar structure of the session was abandoned and the group found themselves in a situation where they had to work out a way of being creative together without any lead or direction from one of the adults. It is difficult to describe how their ideas evolved, because it all happened very quickly like a speeded-up film. The boxes were carried outside onto the lawn and so were scissors and parcel tape. Their first idea was to 'construct something', but they couldn't agree on what to make.
"Let's make an obstacle course!" said someone.

This seemed to immediately ignite their collective imagination. The first idea was to simply create a wall of cardboard boxes that stood waist high and was about five feet across. Inevitably the wall was instantly knocked down! However this led to the idea that knocking down and rebuilding this wall could become part of the course. Whilst a couple of the boys worked out the most stable way to keep the wall standing, three of the girls decided that the white plastic garden chairs might be used in some way.

Suzanna found the parcel tape and had the idea that it could be stuck on one chair, unravelled and then stuck on another chair about six or seven feet away and then people could jump over the tape. I don't know if you have used parcel tape; it's brown in colour, about three centimetres wide and very thin. Whilst it's effective as a means of sealing parcels, it's incredibly unwieldy when it's pulled out more than a few inches in length. The tape easily sticks onto itself and can't be pulled apart. Many lengths of tape were abandoned and screwed into little shiny plastic balls, before the 'high jump' was successfully completed. Suzanna, Evie and Mel all tried it out, but when Evie had her turn she knocked the tape and one of the chairs fell over.

The chairs were too lightweight to be stable. So they decided that when anyone was going to attempt the high jump, then there had to be two people prepared to sit on each of the chairs to weight them down.

Suzanna liked playing around with the tape by pulling it out and sticking it on the grass. This then gave her the idea that there could be a 'start line' to the course and she could stick a strip of tape on the lawn to mark it. She called out to the others and they agreed on where the start would be. Suzanna then asked Zac to help her.

Their ideas continued until they had created their obstacles and were ready to run through the course. It included wriggling through the gap between the legs of one of the chairs and throwing and catching a ball as well as running from one obstacle to another. It struck me that the obstacles they created were rather like the very real obstacles to be overcome in their lives; the internal obstacles, the social obstacles between them and others and the obstacles about how other people saw them.

Stepping over the line The tape stuck to the grass was like a metaphor for 'stepping over the line' in life. At times they had felt humiliated, recognising they had gone too far. They knew what 'stepping over the line' felt like; they had recognised it and had been able to think about it in their work in the group. This line was also like playing with boundaries and overcoming difficulties. As teenagers they were ready to break away a little from the security of the family that the usual group structure represented, and have a new experience.

Knocking over the boxes Children with a diagnosis can be put in a box. They themselves can be boxed in by their difficulties, yet might not be sure how to break out. The wall of boxes was like a metaphor for the barriers preventing them from growing and they wanted to knock them down. They did knock them down in the obstacle course, time and time again.

Tape tied between chairs When the youngsters were fumbling around with the tape it reminded me of their awkwardness with each other and how they got tangled in social situations. However, they persisted till the tape became workable for them. Although the tape was easily damaged they discovered it could also be easily repaired just as they were doing in their emerging relationships with other people. The tape was also a metaphor for creating links and connectedness, together with experiencing the value of co-operation through two of them sitting on the chairs while the third took the jump.

Wriggling through the chair As the youngsters wriggled through the tight space of the chair, it reminded me of their determination to push through, taking courage to try new things whatever the struggle. It was as if they were acting out their desire to work in the Friendly Group and to see it through.

Throwing the ball When the ball was thrown back and forth between the youngsters, it was like a metaphor for the reciprocity of relationships. The 'now me' and 'now you' that needs to happen as sometimes someone catches what you mean and throws it back. Sometimes the ball was dropped. Sometimes relationships are dropped. Then the ball was picked up again just as it can be possible to pick up a relationship.

Cheering each other on During the obstacle course, as each of the group took their turn, the rest were cheering them on. It's the encouragement that we receive from others, their understanding and desire for us to succeed and be happy that can help us to keep going and make progress. It is how we all learn to develop the capacity to open up to friendship and be a part of something rather than being on the margins.

Making links and overcoming obstacles For children on the autism spectrum the greatest difficulty is overcoming the emotional obstacles to forming relationships. The activity of the obstacle course was a metaphor for these teenagers' desires to master and overcome the difficulties in their lives, make links with one another and experience that things can be connected.

> **THINGS TO THINK ABOUT**
>
> In the task and target driven world that we currently live in, it's easy to lose sight of the incredible value of stories and using one's imagination. Being creative is what makes us all feel alive and we are often at our most creative when we get 'side tracked' or have a 'spontaneous impulse'. When I ask children what their favourite part of the session has been (often in the *Circle Time* at the end), *making up the story* is most commonly highlighted.
>
> We do a disservice to children on the autism spectrum to think that they don't have the ability to use their imaginations. They have fantastic imaginations! What they are not always good at is sharing their ideas with others. This is because their anxieties can be so intense that they find it difficult to express themselves. In the next chapter we'll meet some children who struggled with expressing feelings, then with the help of the group and the group leaders, found a way through.

I can't say what I feel

Shame

The word shame often conjures up a sense of guilt, of having done something we regret and for which we feel ashamed. This kind of shame comes from inside us, from a place of self-awareness, and in this context can be a driver and a motivator to make reparation with the other person; to reconnect. However if someone shames another person the *recipient* feels shamed, and this is quite a different experience. When one is shamed by someone else it is unexpected, and outside of one's control. We feel disconnected and stranded; reparation then needs to come from the outside, from the other person.

For everyone, feeling shamed affects our instincts and intuition. It blocks the deepest aspects of ourselves and silences us. Shame of this kind creates disconnection. It arises when we are bullied, put down and humiliated. It arises when we feel we are not known or are misunderstood. When we feel shame we feel excruciatingly vulnerable. We feel shut off from others and unable to connect. In order for there to be connection, we need to be able to share that vulnerability and let our true selves be seen, really seen, by someone else.

Self-knowledge comes hard to everyone but it can be particularly hard for children on the autism spectrum. Self-knowledge is about being able to reflect and to think about yourself, noticing how you feel and behave and being able to imagine how others see you. It is 'getting to know' what kind of person you are.

With self-knowledge one can learn how to manage one's emotions better, make more satisfactory relationships and make better life choices. The children who come to the Friendly Group find it difficult to make friends, particularly within their peer group. In the group sessions they will act out the behaviours that prevent them from connecting with others. I have noticed too, that they can feel shamed by others who never consciously intended to shame them. It happens through ignorance and arises out of frustration. Moreover the feeling of being shamed is very threatening and can trigger the *fight, flight* or *freeze* response.

The fight response
WEEK 1 JEZ AND THE KNIFE

We had just finished working on the *storymaking* part of the session and the *choosing time* part was just about to begin when the children can play freely for a short while. My colleague, Jo, went, as usual, straight to the kitchen to fetch the refreshments but was unexpectedly met in the doorway by Jez, who had managed to get in ahead of her. He was holding a small knife and was clearly heading back, having managed to slip quickly into the kitchen unseen.

> *"This is not the Friendly Group area here, Jez. Put the knife away and go back and join the others,"* said Jo, gently and calmly.

Jez, just as calmly, went back to the kitchen drawer to return the knife, before heading back into the room muttering, *"I want to have Patrick castrated in the story!"* The threat, quietly whispered, indicated the level of stress he was probably feeling. Jez then sat on the floor, in front of the bookshelves, with his back to the room. He was silent and I could see there were tears rolling down his cheeks. He blinked them away. He didn't wipe his face. It was as if he didn't want to draw any attention to himself. He was unresponsive when I spoke to him, so I gave him some space. I knew that the story the group were creating just beforehand had agitated him, but I hadn't realised just how much. The rest of the children seemed unaware of what had just happened as they had gone outside to play.

Maybe as you read this it, it may seem shocking or puzzling that I didn't immediately reprimand Jez in some way, for taking the knife. I made this choice because many sensitive or autistic children find it very difficult to express and process their emotions when they feel under threat in any way. The feelings overwhelm them and the *fight* or *flight* response kicks in. As the response behaviours are often inappropriate, it's tempting to tell a child off. A reprimand is often given to children as a way of teaching them appropriate behaviour. However, reprimanding anxious or autistic children can lead to feelings of shame and frustration and even more extreme reactive behaviours, and so the problems only increase. I knew I had to find another way to address the situation that would benefit the whole group. However, with only minutes left to the end of the session, I felt it was important that Jez went home feeling calm and supported. We could work on the children's differences, frustrations and reactions next time.

Jez (11) had only recently joined this mixed group of boys and girls all aged between ten and twelve. He had entered an unsettled group. There was often a charged atmosphere as one of the newer girls Helena (also 11) was in competition with established Patrick (12) to be the 'gang leader'. Patrick was one of the oldest in the group and had been there the longest. At the start of the new school year Patrick had been keen to take on the role of the *elder,* explaining the rules and so on to all the newcomers. However, with his slow processing and limited language skills, fast-thinking Helena was quick to steal the lead role with entertaining comments and stories. Patrick's attempts at regaining his place with witty comments came across as mean and cutting and when it all fell flat he would sit stiffly with his back against the wall, muttering negative comments under his breath.

Both Helena and Patrick were trying to conceal their insecurities, each wanting to be 'top dog'; one through being outrageous and the other by sticking to the rules. As they couldn't face or own the vulnerable aspects of themselves, it seemed as if they were trying, in very different ways, to manage their anxieties by appearing strong and exerting control. The rest of the group allowed this tussle for leadership to be acted out. Why? When groups work together, the ones who are acting out, so to speak, are doing so for the whole group. Everyone has a 'Helena' or a 'Patrick' aspect to themselves, even if they are not consciously aware of it. While Helena and Patrick struggled in their different ways to secure the lead position they were acting for the whole group, as the others were learning from witnessing their struggles.

Then, the following term, Jez came along and the group dynamic changed completely. Jez was tiny and moved like an elf, leaping lightly around, unable to sit still. His speech was jerky and staccato and very difficult to understand, compounded by the fact he used extraordinarily complex and old-fashioned language. When he became aroused, stressed or in the spotlight it was almost impossible to make sense of what he was saying. In the circle he just couldn't sit still. One minute he was doing press-ups in the middle, the next minute he seemed to be throwing his body at the wall behind him. He once even made a quick dash to play the piano for a few seconds and return with equally lightning speed back to the circle when one of the children was talking. He fiddled endlessly with any object he could lay his hands on, which would suddenly be thrown into the air landing precariously near fragile objects or the other children's heads.

On this particular day, Patrick couldn't cope anymore with Jez's interruptions and unpredictable movements. He found the only way to communicate this was through the group's story. The beginning of the story involved the children each selecting two imaginary objects (often with magic powers) to take on a journey. The children would be travelling on a magic carpet. Helena had decided to take an Olaf key ring. Olaf is a character from the Disney film *Frozen*, known by all the children. She explained that if you talked to the key ring then Olaf would appear. One of Jez's objects was a special shapeshifter mask that would allow him to change into other people.

During the story, Helena got Olaf drunk on Pepsi so that he did irresponsible things. Then as the story developed, the other children made Olaf become both a helper and an agitator, before eating a crazy woman that sent him mad. One of the girls sprinkled magical dust over Olaf which she picked up when flying through a cloud. Olaf vomited up the crazy woman and was back to normal again. This didn't last long, as the crazy woman tempted Olaf to drink lots of Pepsi and he became mad again. Further adventures happened before the crazy woman was sent to the kingdom of Hades, after being burnt in a Russian nuclear power plant. At this point in the story, Jez put on his mask to disguise himself as one of the power plant workers, so he could search for an exit for everyone.

Patrick then offered this contribution to the story;

"Because Olaf and Jez are driving us up the wall and round the bend, they both suddenly explode!"

Patrick sat back with a satisfied smile on his face as Jez looked stunned. I wondered if in that moment Jez gained some insight about how he was perceived by Patrick and was shocked by it. It was then Hani's turn to give her ideas. She had taken on the role as the group's 'peacemaker'. She suggested that after the explosion, Jez could return safely as his normal self. What did Jez think? Jez was speechless. Patrick, however, made repeated 'under his breath' remarks about Jez *'always talking'* and *'butting in'*. Someone else in the group then tried to resolve this impasse by suggesting that not only could Jez return safely, but also that Olaf should join the crazy woman in the kingdom of Hades. Jez still said nothing, but it seemed as if the moment of tension had eased. It was a few moments later, at the start of *choosing time*, when Jez slipped into the kitchen. That was when he found the knife and met Jo.

After *choosing time* the children gathered once again in the circle and waited for me to introduce the last part of the session. I paused before speaking, then used a quiet and grave tone of voice to indicate I was about to say something serious.

> *"I can see that Jez is upset about what happened at the end of the story today. I wonder how others feel about this."*

One of those powerfully silent moments followed as the children turned their attention to Jez who, now with red puffy eyes and cheeks, was sitting very still. It seemed as if a moment of understanding had descended and the children were able to work together as they made their comments and shared their feelings. These are the actual words they said, expressed with a heartfelt truthfulness.

> *"Jez, I feel upset to see you upset because you are such a fun and nice person."*
> *"There is not a boring moment with you in the group."*
> *"You are always happy, Jez. You are someone who is always cheerful in the room."*
> *"You are good at saying what you feel."*
> *"Jez you make the group feel alive."*
> *"The circle is not complete without you, Jez."*
> *"You are like the battery of a torch; you light up the room."*

With each contribution, I could see Jez visibly relaxing and drinking in every positive affirmation and so it was with the rest of the group. At the end I invited Jez to say something and this was his reply, expressed in a clear and steady voice.

"I really like the Friendly Group because the people here are understanding."

This 'understanding' that Jez was communicating (not necessarily consciously) was probably that he was beginning to recognise that whatever he did or said, he was still accepted and liked by the others. Moreover he was communicating that he had experienced a connection with them.

Dealing with the fight response
WEEK 2 STANDING ON THE FEELINGS LINE

The following week the children arrived in their usual way, but I noticed there seemed to be an 'edge' to the atmosphere and they were noisy and excitable. I was aware that despite the positive ending of the previous week, the issues over the story had not yet been resolved. I also wondered what kind of a week it had been for them.

Patrick arrived wearing a black woollen balaclava hat that he had pulled over his face. It looked rather menacing. His mother told me that he had been bullied again at school that week (Patrick never openly talked about uncomfortable feelings). When Taylor unwittingly made a comment that offended him, then apologised, Patrick simply muttered, *"I am used to it."* Helena and Dev could not agree who would be the last one to contribute to the story and it was Hani, as usual, who tried to smooth things over with a possible solution. There was a lot of talking over each other; the children were also talking over my colleagues and me, cutting through any coherent strands of the conversation. In fact there was no coherent dialogue. When this kind of 'talking over one another' behaviour happens in a group, it suggests the group has become disturbed and disconnected.

These young people needed help to be able to think and talk about how they were feeling and a practical activity rather than words seemed the best way forward to facilitate this. So I asked the children to move back a little so we could open up the circle. I then unrolled and stuck a line of parcel tape right through the middle, the full length of the room. The tape stuck firmly on the carpeted floor. At one end we placed a small red block and at the other a green block.

> *"You are each going to have a turn to stand on the line to show how **easy or not** it is to say how you feel if someone in the group is troubling or annoying you. The red end indicates you are uncomfortable and can't say how you feel. The green end indicates you are very happy to say how you feel."*

Patrick, now bare headed, keenly volunteered himself to go first and literally stood on the green brick with a grin on his face. *"I can always say what I feel!"* he announced A quick private glance ricocheted between the adults, as we knew how difficult it was for him to express his feelings openly. This show of confidence was simply a defence.

The rest of the children placed themselves roughly in the middle or towards the (uncomfortable) red brick end. Jez stood almost on top of the red brick when it was his turn.

> *"It looks like, for most of you, it is quite difficult to say if someone is troubling you. I can understand this."* I began.

At this, Jez became increasingly agitated and could barely hold up his head. Patrick simply stared in Jez's direction. I then referred to the group's story and reminded Patrick that his comments of the previous week had upset Jez. Maybe he hadn't realised it at the time, because Jez hadn't said anything.

"Jez, I would like you to tell Patrick how you did not like it when he suggested your character should explode in the story," I continued.

Jez flushed and I thought he was going to burst into tears but he didn't. He simply sat there, unable to open his mouth. This is Jez's difficulty. When there is negativity, especially about him, he feels overwhelmed and loses his voice. Today, I wanted to help him to find his voice.

"I understand you are finding this very upsetting and very difficult, Jez," I said gently. Jez gulped and nodded in agreement. I ventured to say a little more.
"In the Friendly Group everyone finds it difficult to say their feelings sometimes, but we are here to support and help one another."

So we sat and waited. It seemed like an eternity, but it was probably no more than half a minute before Jez turned to Patrick and told him he had not liked what Patrick had said in the story. Patrick momentarily stiffened then responded spontaneously with a genuine apology. Jez accepted it. Patrick's posture relaxed and he added that he was glad that was the end of it. This small but genuine exchange of feelings allowed the two boys to connect in a small way. This continued when later the two of them were jumping on the trampoline and laughing together.

Managing to talk about feelings
WEEK 3 MOVING FORWARD TOGETHER
The following week Patrick managed, at last, to share with the group that he was being bullied at school. This was the first time that he had been able to talk in this way. Patrick was also beginning to find his voice.

That same week Jez arrived in a very subdued state. His mother had forewarned me that his grandmother had just died, but she told me that Jez had been adamant that he did not want to say anything in the group. However, after Patrick had spoken, Jez told us he had something to say. The words tumbled out as he spoke of his grandmother's illness, her recent recovery and the shock of her sudden death.

Jez, too, had begun to find his voice and express his upsets and worries. Patrick had paved the way. Patrick then made this surprisingly sophisticated comment and used these actual words: *"You're doing well to contain it,"* he said, with unexpected empathy. Jez gave him a look of appreciation and he smiled warmly. Patrick had listened to Jez's distress and responded in a caring way and this gesture had been heard and accepted. In that moment Patrick had experienced what it felt like to show empathy and know his 'reaching out' had been warmly received.

The flight response
ISAAC'S HUNT FOR TISSUES

This is the story of a completely different group of slightly older children who were all in their early to mid-teens. It was a summer Saturday morning and three of them were suffering badly with hay fever. There was much snuffling and nose blowing and quite soon the box of tissues was used up. My colleague Claire discreetly invited Isaac (14) to go to the toilet, where he could find some spare tissues for himself. Isaac quietly left the room. A little while later he returned empty-handed. He didn't say anything.

When the group broke for *choosing time*, I went out of the room to fetch something. My husband called to me from the office, which is at the top of a flight of stairs, and explained that a boy had come upstairs but had been told firmly that the first floor was out of bounds. He said that the boy made a hasty retreat without any comment.

In a flash, I realised he must have been talking about Isaac and headed speedily back to the group room. I knew that Isaac was a particularly sensitive boy who was terrified of offending anyone, always trying to do the 'right thing' and became upset and frightened if he thought an adult might tell him off. He was also someone who tended to withdraw in moments of perceived threat. I found him, now, sitting stiffly in the corner of the room and staring vacantly, looking rather like a rabbit caught in the headlights.

> *"I've just found out that my husband had a sharp word with you on the stairs just now,"* I said to him gently.
> *"Yes. I couldn't find where the toilet was downstairs, so I went upstairs to look. I'm sorry,"* he said.
> *"Have you never used the toilet here before?"*
> *"No,"* was his response.
> *"Then you have done nothing wrong, Isaac. Let's go upstairs together and you can explain this to my husband."*

Isaac retraced his steps and I followed him. He managed to say why he had come up the stairs and my husband responded with these words.

> *"I am so sorry if I sounded a bit harsh. I didn't realise you were looking for the toilet. Younger children have sometimes tried coming upstairs just to explore. I hope you will forgive me."*

What followed was a relaxed exchange between the two of them. Once Isaac came down the stairs he turned to me and said, *"If I had been able to say I didn't know where the loo was in the first place, then this would have never happened."* I agreed, reassuring him that it is good to speak up in the first place as it can prevent misunderstandings or things possibly going wrong later.

At the end of the session Isaac shared with the group that the best bit of the morning had been the encounter on the stairs! What children discover, time and time again, is that when they are able to face and talk about those difficult moments, they feel really good about themselves afterwards. In this particular instance, what was also important for Isaac was that he had the experience of an adult apologising. This adult had recognised he had spoken in an unnecessarily harsh manner and had asked Isaac for forgiveness. Isaac had accepted. So often, children like Isaac build up inner resentments when there have been misunderstandings that have not been sorted out and talked about at the time. Parents have often shared stories of their children telling them, in a moment of anger, that they still haven't forgiven them for something like *'not letting them have the chocolate ice cream on a holiday five years ago!'*

There was synchronicity at work that morning too. The group had been read a short story, the theme of which was all about forgiveness. For Isaac, the story had not been simply theoretical but an actual here-and-now experience. Isaac was able to talk about his feelings and this opened up the opportunity for others to share some of their experiences too. When the children can talk in this way it allows their inner strength to develop and their resilience to deepen.

The freeze response
SNIGGERING TEENAGERS

The summer holiday group was in full swing. Every year, at the end of July, 10 to 12 children from any of the four groups can come for a whole morning each day for a week. Much of the morning is like an extended *choosing time*, where there are extra resources like a large climbing frame, dressing-up clothes, boxes, parcel tape, blankets and so on.

One of these years, two of the well-established boys, now aged 14, had recently started that awkward and self-conscious transition towards adolescence. On arrival they kept at a distance from the younger children, by sitting on the top of the climbing frame, whispering and sniggering together. Normally they would soon have joined in or led the play with the others, but the appearance of two rather attractive girls (both 13), whom they had not met before, diverted their attention. The two girls who had befriended one another from another group made a beeline for the boys. Sitting on top of the frame the four of them 'flirted' with one another, probably feeling they were beyond the reach and notice of the adults and other children.

However, one of the girls, Inger, soon left the other three in their huddle, attracted by the arrival of blankets, boxes, string and scissors, brought in by a young adult assistant. Soon, her teenage posturing evaporated as she discovered a creative ally in the form of Taylor (11). From then on, she and Taylor spent much of the week initiating play with the other children in all manner of things including making a camp, storytelling and creating an obstacle course.

Each day during refreshment time, when all 12 children were sitting round the large table together, I would encourage them to talk about how they felt about the morning so far. I would ask them to identify who had been kind or a good friend. I also reminded them that if something went wrong, or they were upset by anything or anyone, it was important to speak out and say something, seeking the adults if necessary.

"You know that the adults here will never shout at you and together we can sort out any problems."

This particular group quickly settled and found different ways to play and spend their time. However, I noticed that the 'teenage threesome' continued to sit apart and whisper and snigger. It created an 'us and them' feel about the group. At one point, two of the younger boys started to roll around on the trampoline taking turns to show each other their tricks. This was the first time that these two boys had played together in this way and their laughter suggested that they were both enjoying the experience.

I then became aware that they were being mockingly jeered by the three teenagers. I decided to step in and let the teenagers know that this had not gone unnoticed and what they were doing was unacceptable. I went up to them. I did not make direct eye contact as this could have felt threatening, but stood close enough to indicate that I was going to speak.

"You can have your own private conversations," I said, *"but it's unkind to laugh at what others are doing. Please think how you would feel if people were laughing like that at you."*

They nodded and when I also added, *"You all know how it feels to be laughed at and made fun of,"* they agreed, but nevertheless found it difficult to contain their sniggering. The three of them didn't know how to be accepting or playful with the other children without losing face with each other. They were actually behaving like most adolescents.

What is sniggering about? We all know what it is: we have witnessed it or experienced it or done it ourselves. Sniggering is associated with fear and trying to fit in with a peer group with whom you feel unsure and yet also look up to. It happens when the behaviour of someone (or another group) makes you cringe. This is because you recognise something of yourself there that you don't want to admit to others or maybe even yourself. There's conflict inside you. It's an unconscious attempt to look bigger, greater or more mature with others with whom you're trying to fit in, while unconsciously identifying with the 'embarrassing' behaviour being acted out by someone else.

It occurred to me that here in the group the making of rude (and often sexualised) comments, goading each other about their sexuality, laughing at others' behaviour and play was probably this threesome's immature way of expressing their own emerging sexuality. They were becoming more self-conscious about themselves. At home and at school they were still seen as largely innocent and childlike. However, in this safe environment, where there was an element of freedom and perceived privacy, they could experiment with their different persona and their departure from childhood. However, it was my responsibility as the adult to also guide the youngsters away from potential cruelty and towards empathy and understanding. Here is another story from that group.

Being laughed at and goaded

During the week, if you remember, Inger, while initially interested in the two teenage boys, had in fact immersed much of her time in creative activity with a younger boy called Taylor. From time to time she would leave him and nudge her way into the teenage huddle for a little while before bursting out and continuing her play. At one of the times that she joined the teenagers she sat close to Kylian and, without any warning, asked him if he would like to be her boyfriend. At age 13, her idea of a boyfriend was probably rather innocent and immature. Kylian, though, looked shocked. I knew from his parents that he talked of wanting a girlfriend one day, but an approach of this kind had never happened to him before and he flushed with embarrassment. The other two began laughing but Kylian, like most children on the autism spectrum, probably took Inger's request very seriously and didn't know how to answer her. In this perplexed state, he simply froze and became silent. The other two began to press him to give an answer. This new development was probably exciting for them, but as they goaded him on I wondered if Kylian was becoming stressed.

He climbed down from the tower and approached me, explaining what had happened and said he felt frustrated and didn't like to be put under pressure. I acknowledged his feelings and encouraged him to tell the others how he felt. However it seemed that shock and anxiety had overwhelmed him, as he was unable to speak before the close of the session. He simply froze. I decided we would work on it the next day. I wondered how the others were feeling, and if they realised how upset and frustrated Kylian was.

Next morning, before the session formally started and out of sight of the younger children, I invited the teenagers to sit round the table in the back room. I didn't have to say much by way of introduction, as they seemed to guess why we were there. In the safety and privacy of this much smaller group, Kylian was able to speak.

"I'm a serious boy and I don't like being put under pressure. When you kept questioning me yesterday and pushing me to give an answer, I didn't like it. It made me very frustrated. I told my dad about it last night and he said I should forgive you so I have. Forgive and forget is what I say!"

The supportive and apologetic, albeit embarrassed response was spontaneous and created a much needed release for all of them. Shortly afterwards, Kylian joined in with some of the younger children, allowing his playful side full expression once again. This gave the others an opening to join in the play too. Later that morning Kylian was able to tell Inger that although he liked her, he wasn't ready to have a girlfriend. She accepted this in a matter-of-fact manner and simply continued with what she was doing; the planning of a den within the climbing tower, for the whole group. During the closing part of the session when there was time for shared reflection Kylian, without hesitation, asked to speak first.

"I have learnt how speak up for myself and say how I feel. I have also learnt how to forgive and it all feels good."

The shadow side of our nature

Adolescence is a minefield of misunderstanding, misjudgement and mistreatment. As youngsters become more aware of family and cultural norms and expectations, they begin to wonder about what kind of people they would like to become. They are curious and want to experiment with how it feels to think and behave differently from their families. What they are doing is trying out different persona which Robert A. Johnson (1991) aptly describes as one's 'psychological clothing'. Indeed adolescents also make conscious use of fashion as physical props to express their persona and indicate the group with whom they want to associate, such as hipsters, punks, Emos, nerds and geeks, to name but a few.

We all have different persona within us, some of which we don't like and so try to hide them. More importantly there are hidden aspects that *we don't even realise we are hiding*, and these are described as the 'shadow'. The shadow aspects can be of both good and bad qualities. These shadow aspects of oneself are about those *unacknowledged parts of one's identity or personality*. You may not even be aware of them as they remain unconscious. Others may not be aware of your shadow either. Yet, this is not always the case. Your shadow may be visible and known to others, even though it's hidden from you. It was the psychologist, Carl Jung, who first used this term, but his insight is often interpreted too simplistically, with the shadow being understood as simply our bad or 'dark' sides. This isn't correct; the shadow also refers to our creative and courageous sides too.

A sensitive and naturally quiet boy may portray himself as crude and jocular to fit in with a masculine peer group, or an intelligent woman may conceal her competence with frivolous comments in order to avoid undermining her less intelligent male partner. At certain times, such behaviours can be useful to be able to fit in and make relationships work. However, when one's shadow aspect is ignored, life gets out of balance and disturbance follows. I was once talking to a monk who confessed that he enjoyed reading thrillers. He didn't like to openly admit this fact, as his rational mind told him that a monk shouldn't be reading about death and killing. However his wise intuitive mind was guiding him to strike a much needed balance between the life-affirming spiritual aspects of his life and some of life's brutish and earthy aspects. He did this through reading fiction as well as religious works.

In the Friendly Group there is the opportunity for children and young people to not only become more aware of the different facets of their persona, but to appreciate and enjoy them. On many occasions I have, for example, witnessed a timid child discover courage, and a serious child delight in expressing humour. As Socrates said, *"An unexamined life is a life not worth living."* The journey towards happiness and fulfilment involves taking a good look at oneself over and over, 'warts and all'. However, if we simply engage in self-examination we can dive too deeply into a well of negativity or become unhealthily preoccupied with ourselves. We need companions and helping hands along the way to help us recognise, experience and accept our multi-faceted selves. The Friendly Group offers that companionship and those helping hands as the children inch their way together towards better self-awareness, and discover how to express the various aspects of their personalities in a balanced, conscious and comfortable way.

THINGS TO THINK ABOUT

When we feel threatened or shamed it creates high levels of anxiety. We feel terrified and can't think, so we just react. And the three reactions (or responses) are the 'fight', 'flight' and 'freeze' responses. I have seen these responses time and time again in children both in the Friendly Group and in numerous other contexts.

Perhaps you have seen them at home with your children, or in your workplace with children or young people? These reactions to threat are normal, whether we have special needs or not. However, if you can help children to learn to say how they are feeling, at the time when they are simply feeling 'uncomfortable', this will not only help them to manage their anxieties better but will also help them to gain self-confidence and to increase their success in making friendships.

CHAPTER 13

The issue of bullying and the opportunity for growth

Vulnerability, aggression and assertiveness

Bullying is something that can emerge in any group at one time or another. We seem to be in a bullying culture at the moment, which is divisive and dangerous. When someone is a bully or feels a victim of bullying they are probably reacting to a perceived threat.

Being a victim and the bullying behaviour are really two aspects of the same experience: vulnerability. In order to find our strength we need to learn how to be assertive, part of the necessary process of separating ourselves from others and standing on our own feet. However there are those who feel that the only way to show they are assertive is by bullying and being aggressive. It looks strong. When they see someone who looks vulnerable it reminds them of their own vulnerability, which they don't want to acknowledge, since it makes them feel uncomfortable. So what seems the only way to get rid of these uncomfortable feelings? Hurting someone. They feel compelled to hurt the vulnerable one as a way of unconsciously telling themselves, "They're not like me. I'm strong." However, this is a false voice.

Meanwhile, the one who is the victim and unable to stand up for him or herself has no voice (yet), and is too weak to be convincing. While this continues, vulnerability on both sides is reinforced. What's needed is for the sensitive victim to find his strong voice and the aggressive bully to find his sensitive voice. In this way they are both expressing strength and authenticity and are learning to be assertive.

Children on the autism spectrum are vulnerable to bullying on two counts. Firstly, they often don't understand how their behaviour might impact on another person, and secondly, they are particularly sensitive to taking things personally. Let me tell you about what happened to Matt.

MATT'S STORY AND THE QUESTION OF REASSURANCE

Matt (13) arrived much earlier than usual and came into the group room looking rather tense. There was sweat on his face and his lips were quivering. Matt had recently transferred to a teenagers' group, where over half of the youngsters were completely new to him.

Whilst Matt had been gaining in confidence and was positive about this move to a new group, he remained unable to talk openly about any of his problems. Instead, he took on the role of the listener. He preferred to offer listening support to someone else rather than seek support for himself. I knew from meetings over the years with his parents that he had great difficulty managing his anxieties and often had angry outbursts and meltdowns at home when things got too much for him. He occasionally expressed his worries in quiet conversations with me, but these were short and away from the group. He struggled to think about his uncomfortable feelings and kept his worries private.

On this occasion, seeing there was no-one else in the room Matt began to talk to me.

> *"I need to tell you something very personal Anita,"* he began with a tone of urgency, *"I was bullied yesterday."*
>
> *"I can see you still seem rather shaky Matt. Let's sit down here together."*

I made it clear that there was plenty of time to talk, as the other young people weren't due for a little while. Matt explained that he had arrived especially early so he could talk to me on his own.

"It happened yesterday on the way home in the taxi," he began.

Matt attended a special school for children with learning difficulties and had a daily one hour journey each way in school transport with three other teenage boys who were a couple of years older than him.

"Normally the other boys in the taxi are just loud and silly but yesterday they were really mean to me. They were laughing and kept saying nasty things. I asked them to stop but they just went on and on and I got really upset," he said with a tremor in his voice.

ALTERNATIVE WAYS FORWARD

Matt's distress was palpable and I wanted to help him but had to think about how best to do this. It would have been easy to try and reassure Matt by saying something like, *"Well at least you are here with us, now, Matt. You are back with your friends. That incident is all over and I expect your Mum can talk to the school and sort things out."* Matt would have probably smiled and nodded in agreement, feeling momentarily relieved, but inside his distress would have been suppressed and not resolved.

I might have made a special effort to give Matt a fun time in the session to try and cheer him up. I could have said no more about the bullying incident. However, I knew that if I took those courses of action it might have reassured *me* that *I* was being the supportive and helpful adult, but it would have been denying Matt the opportunity to think about what had happened to him and to learn and grow from it. If, at that moment, I had succumbed to the urge to be helpful and reassuring it would have been a sign that Matt's distress was getting to me, triggered by either my feelings of helplessness or related to my own unresolved difficulties.

It's very easy when we find ourselves agitated by someone else's upset to resort to comforting platitudes, but when this happens the opportunity for that individual's growth is lost. Indeed, all therapy is, at heart, about being able to tolerate someone expressing their distress and experiencing the paradox of allowing oneself to feel that other person's pain, which seems to feel unbearable, and yet also be able think about it, and bear it alongside them, so that they find their own way through.

When I heard Matt tell his story and when I saw his flushed face I felt his rising distress and I was momentarily in that taxi with him. I felt a rush of maternal protection and defensive indignation rise inside me. However, I knew I needed to stand back from this emotional response, that desire to 'make it better', and find the words to reach Matt from an empathic place. I would only be able to support him to bear it if I translated his experience into words or gestures that he could accept. The first step was to acknowledge his feelings.

> *"That was probably very difficult for you Matt, because you couldn't get away from those boys in the taxi. I know you're good about walking away when other people say unkind remarks,"* I said, and Matt looked at me intently with an expression that suggested relief that I had understood.

Matt's parents had told me on several occasions since Matt started the group that he had difficulty coping when people were laughing around him. This perplexed me as he had seemed to cope well when there was laughter in the Friendly Group. I wondered if he was anxious about being *laughed at*, or if laughter was simply a noise that was too loud for him. I wondered if he had had a negative experience at an early age, and the laughter triggered an old stress response. I wondered if the boys in the taxi were simply being noisy and boisterous. However, Matt began to tell me more.

> *"That was the trouble, I was stuck in the taxi and they kept saying these nasty things about my mum."*
> *"No wonder you are so upset Matt. That is one of the most hurtful things anyone can do,"* I added.
> *"Is it?"* asked Matt. He seemed curious as to what I would say next, so I continued.
> *"If someone says something unkind to you, it hurts inside, but when you're feeling generally confident you learn to cope."* Matt nodded.
> *"But if someone really wants to hurt someone else's feelings, they say unkind things about their mother. Listen to arguments in the playground at school. You'll find that usually the most upsetting things are about someone's mum."*
> *"I didn't realise that,"* said Matt, already relaxing his shoulders and speaking with a stronger voice.

I am aware, from my experience of listening to teenagers in school settings, that they can be crude in their insults and use very hurtful language. Often their last resort is to make unkind comments about the mother of the one they are insulting. Matt looked both shocked and relieved when I explained this to him, because that was precisely what had happened and he told me the very words the other boys used. I asked him how he had reacted, and he explained he'd kept quiet on the journey but when he got home he became very angry and upset. What had made it even worse was that his mother had got upset and was very angry about the other boys too.

> *"No wonder you got angry and upset Matt. I can imagine it must have been frightening to see your mum so upset too. But the comments those boys made about your mother weren't really about her."*
>
> *"What do you mean?"* asked Matt, looking confused.
>
> *"Well, do these boys know your mum?"* I asked.
>
> *"No, they don't,"* was his reply.
>
> *"So whatever comments they made weren't about your mum at all. They were comments that these boys knew would really upset you. When people say mean things about someone we love, it's very upsetting."*

This idea seemed a revelation to Matt and he actually smiled for a moment. I then decided to go one step further.

> *"Perhaps these boys were saying the very things to you that other people might have said to them about their mothers?"*

I spoke slowly and deliberately, emphasising certain words so that Matt might understand what I was saying. He continued to listen. I then went on to ask if there had been any other adults in the taxi with the driver and what these people had said or done.

> *"They didn't do anything, Anita! They told the boys to quieten down but they just ignored the driver and the lady. They seemed frightened of the boys like I was."*

Our conversation ended as I could see a couple of the other youngsters from the group arriving. I asked Matt if he'd be prepared to talk about his experience in the session. He shook his head at first, but then agreed that he would.

MATT'S GROUP BEGINS TO MATURE

When Matt began to share his experiences with the rest of the group he went red in the face. His voice became rather high pitched and he coughed several times. The group sat in complete silence as Matt told his story. He gave a sigh and his shoulders fell when he had finished. It was the first time that Matt had been able to give a coherent narrative about a personal experience. It was time for the adults to stay quiet and let the other children respond.

> *"That's happened to me,"* said Wayne, (13) *"I know how you feel. I think you need to get help from someone. Can you take an iPod or something in the taxi and listen to music?"*

Wayne was able to acknowledge Matt's feelings because he had also been bullied and knew how it felt. His comments suggested that Matt's story had touched and disturbed him. What followed was an outpouring from various group members about their experiences of being bullied. Genuine connections were being made between the children as they responded empathically, repeating comments like, *"That's happened to me"* or *"I know how you feel"*. Whilst they offered some advice, as Wayne did, they mostly focussed on their experience and empathising with Matt, not problem-solving. Instead of the talk being about the 'content' of Matt's story, it had now come into 'process', meaning the here-and-now of the 'shared feelings' in the group. This is another example of group process which facilitates learning and group cohesion as I describe in Chapter 6.

DISCOVERING INNER STRENGTH

The following week Matt updated the group about his taxi experiences. The boys in question were no longer bothering him in the taxi. He explained that his mum had spoken to the school and, as he put it, *'The situation has been sorted'*. This was a typical story I'd heard many times before. The adults in Matt's life had taken charge of the situation and acted for him. It's necessary for children and young people to be able to seek out adult help and support. However, within that support, opportunities need to be provided for that individual to be able to think about what has happened and to do something about it for themselves. In this way they develop resilience, discover their inner strengths and can grow from them. When adults simply take over however, vulnerabilities can be reinforced.

Matt's experience offered an opportunity not only for his own development, but for the development of the group as a whole. My colleagues and I knew that all the children in the group had been bullied or picked on at one time or another. They reacted in different ways to provocation, from hitting others to running away and hiding. Their experiences were remembered in 'technicolour detail' and they held onto their fears and resentments. They found it almost impossible to see what had happened to them from the 'bully's' point of view, stuck in their egocentric way of thinking. We decided to introduce some roleplay using the taxi scenario which Matt had described.

Roleplay can be very effective, especially with teenagers, as they can 'try out' different ways of behaving in a safe environment. Once the initial embarrassment of selecting players and acting in role had been overcome, I invited the group to roleplay Matt's taxi experience. It was decided that Matt would play one of the bullies and Jacob offered to play the role of Matt. No-one else wanted to play the bully role. They said it felt all wrong and they didn't want to hurt Matt's feelings.

> *"You won't hurt my feelings,"* said Matt and with further encouragement, Wayne and Eden came forward.
>
> The four players arranged themselves as if they were in a taxi. The rest of us watched. It didn't take long for Matt to start playing the part.
>
> *"You're weird! "* he said tentatively, facing Jacob's back. Jacob, playing the role of Matt, was sitting in the front of the imagined vehicle.
>
> *"That's it!"* I encouraged, seeing Matt shrinking from the role, *"What you're saying is brilliant ... come on, be that bully, what else did he say?"*

Matt slowly began to gain in confidence. He sat up and his voice became steadily louder and stronger.

> *"You're a nerd!"* he shouted, *"You're just a Mummy's boy."*

I encouraged the other 'bullies' to speak but they just couldn't find the words. Instead, Wayne began poking Jacob. Eventually Eden did make one or two rude comments. Jacob didn't react so Wayne poked him even harder in the shoulder and Matt (playing one of the bullies) joined in. Jacob played out the role (of Matt) brilliantly and kept quiet; his body shrinking with every insult. Meanwhile Matt's energy had really been fired up and he was uttering swear words and insults in a way that I couldn't have imagined he'd be able to do in front of the group.

> *"That felt really weird acting as bully. I'm just not like that in real life,"* said Matt, after the roleplay was over.

Jacob, playing the role of Matt, and who was generally a more volatile boy, had this to say of the experience.

"And I normally get angry," said Jacob, *"But I was trying to be like you Matt. The way you were poking my back, Wayne, made me feel upset. And people were saying such horrible stuff. Matt! I bet you were really upset when it happened to you."*

"I was," agreed Matt.

"They just say those things to be offensive," added Wayne, *"but it feels all wrong to me."*

"I think bullies have a tiny piece somewhere that feels guilty. They just want a reaction," commented Jacob as he reflected on the experience.

I then invited them to repeat the role-play. However, this time Matt was to be himself and act as he would have liked to have responded; from the strong part of himself. There were new players in the bully role but once again they were reluctant to play their parts. Matt turned round (from his imagined front seat of the taxi) to face the three boys playing the bully role, and reassured them, saying, *"It's okay! You can be as mean as you like. I know it's not real. We are only acting. You can't hurt me."*

It took a few moments before the scene got going, but soon Matt was being prodded and poked and the insults came pouring out. The boys playing the bully role knew the language. They had had these insults slung at them in the past and it was all very familiar to them. They had sometimes behaved like that themselves.

This time, what was very different was that Matt in role not only sat tall and even seemed to puff out his chest, he also shrugged his shoulders in a purposeful and confident manner whenever he was prodded or poked. He turned round from time to time and said, *"Just leave me alone, will you."* His voice was clear, loud and assertive. When the role-play came to an end the observers were quick to comment on how confident Matt seemed. *"I wonder how that felt this time Matt,"* I invited.

> *"It was interesting,"* he said, smiling and looking very happy indeed. *"It felt different ... very different. I felt more confident in the situation."*

Christopher, who had also played one of the bullies, told the group he'd been worried that he might have taken it too far, as he knew that he had it in him to do so. Rick said that he too was worried he might have offended the others.

> *"Did you notice the way Matt shook us off?"* asked Christopher. *"He just shook us off without any reaction. It felt like he didn't respect me. I felt like a bug being shrugged off."*

The role-play had not only given the boys an opportunity to see what it feels like to stand up against bullying, but also an insight into the power of the assertive voice. They had a flavour of the vulnerability of the 'bully' and the strength of the 'victim' and the way they are really two sides of the same thing; the need to discover one's own identity.

The experience also made a big impression on them as a group, and contributed to the group becoming very close. It created a memorable experience to which they returned from time to time. Matt returned to school and began to find his voice and stand up to the low-level bullying. He was also able to share these personal developments with his peers, further reinforcing his confidence and awareness of the strengths inside him.

Trolling and cyber-bullying

Before Matt joined this group it had gone through a very difficult period. The teenagers had struggled to gel and trust each other, creating a lot of turbulence and distrust within the group. They had got stuck in a place where winning approval with peers meant being very negative and provocative, but this only served to divide and unsettle the group even further.

My colleagues, Claire and Gaby and I also felt stuck, and this is what I wrote in one of my reflective notes after a particularly negative session.

> *What a terrible session. Claire said it was her 'worst week ever'. Gaby and I shared that we had felt a real coldness. The atmosphere was so negative and disconnected. There was no kindness or consideration between any of them today. Jacob kept expressing indignation and anger. Darren said he had no feeling whatsoever about school. In fact he said "I feel blank. The only way I can describe it is like a heart monitor that has gone flat." Christopher said he couldn't be bothered with anything. I am left feeling cold and disheartened. I have an odd shuddering feeling too because Jacob then threw in a comment that I don't understand. He said, "When I get bored I troll people online." What does that mean? Claire thinks it might be some kind of online bullying. I must look this up."*

This was several years ago when online bullying was not in the general domain. At the time I decided to look up the definition of the word 'trolling' on Wikipedia:

> In internet slang, a troll is a person who sows discord on the Internet by starting arguments or upsetting people, by posting inflammatory, extraneous or off-topic messages in an online community (such as a forum, chat room or blog), either accidentally or with deliberate intent of provoking readers into an emotional response or of otherwise disrupting normal on-topic discussion. Media attention in recent years has equated trolling with online harassment.

So trolling is a form of online bullying or cyber bullying. There are numerous cases of young people and adults traumatised, even to the point of suicide, following this kind of 'remote bullying'. Bullying creates its own problems when children and teenagers are in face-to-face social situations, but an online situation can create a whole range of other problems when an individual doesn't necessarily know with whom they are communicating.

When someone makes a cruel comment or takes aggressive action online and they don't see the other person, it becomes possible to be even more unkind and aggressive than if they are seeing a person face-to-face, a kind of cold-blooded cruelty. You can treat someone as if they don't bleed or hurt because in the virtual online world they become a 'disembodied other'. They're not imagined as a living breathing person. I almost see a parallel between online bullying and someone leaving a bomb to explode in a public place.

My colleague Claire had heard two of the boys discussing 'trolling' in *choosing time* and they seemed to be revelling in what they saw as the funny side of the whole thing. They were clearly interpreting trolling as playing innocent pranks online, and didn't appreciate the seriousness of engaging in such activity. I wanted to be able to open up the possibility for the group to talk and reflect on this subject, both to increase their awareness and reduce their vulnerability. I also saw it as an opportunity to help strengthen the group.

> *"Last week I overheard someone in the group mention something called trolling,"* I began. *"I hadn't heard of this word before and wondered if any of the rest of you know what this is."*

I could see Jacob's body immediately tense and he averted his gaze. This feeling of tension then rippled around some other members of the group. I had struck a nerve.

Christopher was the first to speak explaining it through a computer game.

> *"It's when you do a prank at someone else's expense that they will find funny in the end. Like setting a trap in Minecraft and shouting 'troll'!"*
> *"But you can roll back on Minecraft. You can undo the troll by typing in 'roll back'. I know you can get banned from servers for 'griefing'. That's destroying others' property,"* interjected Jacob talking in the jargon of the computer world. His tone was defensive.
> *"Some people don't have the facility of 'roll back' on their computers, though,"* said Eden.
> *"Trolling is fun. It's not mean,"* added Christopher who was picking up on the charged atmosphere.
> *"Trolling is basically 'schadenfreude',"* said Eden, *"taking pleasure in someone else's anger. It's more like a prank that's gone too far."* He often spoke with intellectual confidence and used a wide range of vocabulary.
> *"Well I would say that it's only doing extremely annoying pranks,"* said Rick, *"But they are only funny to the person who does the trolling."*
> *"I would say that it's a bit like 'chat-roulette' because you speak to people you don't know,"* continued Christopher.

When each of them had had an opportunity to speak, it was time to say something myself. I told them that I had looked up the meaning of the word and would share it with them. Trolling is -

- sending messages which are grossly offensive
- an offence - several people have been imprisoned for trolling
- an activity that requires deceiving someone

- treating someone as if they didn't hurt
- purposefully antagonising people

Christopher was quick to point out that it was only adults who had been imprisoned and queried whether deceiving was actually good or bad. Christopher was the one who had said that trolling was fun: his resorting to factual knowledge seemed to me to be a form of defence. *"I want to change the subject! It's boring! "* announced Eden, suggesting that he didn't know how to deal with his feelings other than to challenge me.

"This is getting awkward," commented Rick.
"I think you are telling us all off," said Christopher.

I responded by saying that I wasn't telling them off, but that perhaps it felt like it to them. I wondered if they had a sense that the behaviour they were describing had a reprehensible quality to it and whether Christopher's comment reflected some kind of defensive guilt. Maybe my response sounded rather defensive and I could have said something like, *"I wonder what is making you think I am telling you off?"* keeping the dialogue in the here-and-now. However, at the time I felt I needed to continue with the subject matter as a way of closing things down before the end of the session. I concluded by saying that this was a serious subject that affected everyone and it was good that they had been able to talk so openly. I also explained that it was important to think about the difference between playing a prank on someone, who is there with you and whom you would consider a friend, and playing what might seem like a prank on someone whom you might not know and whose reaction you cannot see.

Usually the boys from this group never shared what had been discussed with their parents. However, on this occasion three of them immediately brought up the subject on their way home. At an evening parents' session soon after, I was told that this had opened up a very useful conversation with their children, for which they were very grateful. Some parents were unaware of trolling or cyber bullying and found it helpful to learn about it. Following this session the group steadily began to settle, but it took some months before they really began to relax and trust one another. When they did, they became an exceptionally happy and supportive group.

It is important to engage autistic children and teenagers in this subject because they are both technically competent yet emotionally naïve. Some recent cases of hacking data and inciting violence over social media and the internet, which have been brought to the judicial system, have involved people with Asperger's Syndrome or autism. They are viewed as very serious offences and an Autism Spectrum Disorder diagnosis does not necessarily protect someone from being prosecuted.

Turning a serious incident upside down with humour

I was reminded of another group and how they had responded to the invitation to role-play a bullying incident. This was a well-established group of 12-14 year olds who enjoyed a lot of shared humour and banter. Hugo (14) was someone who always provided entertaining stories and appeared very confident on the outside. However, I wondered if this compulsion to entertain was a defence against opening up and sharing his vulnerable feelings. It was his mother who had alerted me to the bullying that Hugo was experiencing on his walk home after school. She asked if I could in some way bring this into the group. I used the *Bear Cards* to facilitate this.

> *"Choose a bear card that illustrates how you feel when something frightening is happening,"* I suggested.

When it was Hugo's turn, he was able to share his experience of being physically assaulted by a small group of 16-year-old boys in an underpass and how his rucksack had been pulled off him and thrown away. Luckily he had managed to find and retrieve it later. Hugo's story shocked the other young people. When I suggested that they could roleplay the incident the group did it in the way that suited them; by making the scene into a comedy.

They decided that one of the other children would be the rucksack! So a smaller member climbed onto Hugo's back and the scene was re-enacted this way. It dissolved into play fighting and laughter, enabling them to process the seriousness of the incident in a safe way. They then used their imaginations to re-enact other similar experiences, which showed Hugo he wasn't alone. The role-play on that day strengthened group cohesion, as well as Hugo's self-confidence.

We can all be bullies

Developmental progress involves facing our fears and the dark sides of ourselves. This chapter has largely focused on children who have been on the receiving end of bullying, but these same children are equally capable of bullying others. I would like to conclude this chapter by telling Philip's story.

Many children on the autism spectrum have a tendency to stick rigidly to rules, which can result in them behaving like little 'policemen', pointing out others' misdemeanours or errors. This not only alienates them socially but can also lead to inappropriate and sometimes cruel behaviour. Philip (15) was the eldest of three brothers and his efforts to control his younger siblings were a torment for them. His way of policing them was to fight with them, but he was a lot bigger than them and he didn't realise how much he could hurt them. He felt they *'deserved their punishments'*. His parents were at their wits' end. In the group Philip was mild mannered and always had words of advice for the other members of the group, who were rather in awe of him. However, the advice-giving seemed to be a shield for

Philip to hide behind. He preferred helping others rather than sharing his own fears and worries. One day Philip had a transformative experience. For the first time, he spontaneously brought a 'worry' to the group.

> *"I don't know how to tell you this,"* he began, *"but I got in a terrible fight last weekend with a younger boy and it has really scared me. I feel really bad."*
> *"It's difficult to share something that is scary,"* I acknowledged.
> *"My family and I were at this football BBQ thing and we were in a field. My brothers go to football and I had to look after some of the younger boys. Well one of them was being silly, and I told him off but he didn't listen to me. He ran off into some woods and I chased him … and then,"* Philip swallowed and found it difficult to get the words out: *"I beat him up. I was punching him and punching him. I don't know what had got into me. I couldn't stop. And I hurt him. The other boys ran to get my parents. I got into a lot of trouble. But I feel awful that I could hurt a boy like that. And he was younger than me and he was absolutely terrified."*

From the moment Philip had told his story, something in him seemed to change. When children stick to the narrow, *'I'm right and you're wrong'* script, they inhabit a restricted world. However, when Philip told his story, dramatic though it was, he seemed to soften and it became a humbling and enlightening experience for him. Philip had witnessed on previous occasions that the Friendly Group was a place where the other children and adults don't judge you, but when he told his own story, he experienced for himself the healing of group acceptance. In re-telling the story he probably began to realise that he was like everyone else; he could treat others badly at times and regretted it. When children experience this realisation, change can happen quickly inside and they discover the world can be a more generous place. Philip had also been able to face himself, and stand back, conscious of how he had behaved and how it had affected others. The telling of his story allowed him to reflect and in so doing he had begun to mature. Following this session, Philip quickly began to respond to his siblings as an older brother, and become a positive role model for them.

I'd like to conclude this chapter by sharing a more recent group's joint definition of bullying. This group was comprised of eight 12-15-year-old boys and girls. They wrote their ideas on a whiteboard during one of the sessions. Below are the exact words they used.

BULLYING - WHAT IS IT?
- When someone is continuously not being nice to you
- It can start off as teasing but becomes more serious if it carries on
- There can be a reason for bullying; it can take away the pain if you are very unhappy
- Bullying can lead to retaliation but that makes everything worse
- Bullying can be physical as well as using words and the words can be behind your back
- A bully is someone who is a pain in the backside; annoying
- Bullying is a repeated form of behaviour intended to hurt someone physically or emotionally
- Bullying can be about leaving someone out, exclusion

THINGS TO THINK ABOUT

Maybe you have been a bully at some point in your life? Maybe you were a victim of bullying at school? Maybe your child is being bullied at school? Maybe there's been bullying in the school you work at?

Bullying behaviour makes us feel upset, frightened and angry and we can often want to blame someone else. There can be a tendency to use the term 'bullying' to describe general unkindness or vindictive behaviour, but this distorts the meaning. We can all be unkind and vindictive at times, but bullying is when a behaviour persists and is targetted at a particular person or group. We need to remember that while bullying is behaviour that is deliberate and intended to hurt someone else, it usually springs from deep hurt and vulnerability.

CHAPTER 14

Stuck in transition

Imagine this

Imagine it's the morning and you're lying in bed. You know you've got to get up but you don't want to. It's warm and cosy and you're still half asleep. You turn over. Maybe you can give yourself just five more minutes?

You don't want to face the day with all its challenges; the quarrelling children, the traffic on the road, the hostile boss, that pile of reports, endless emails or even simply the cold air against your body as you emerge from the covers.

But you do get out of bed! You make that transition from the cosy nest that is bed to whatever the day will bring. You can do this because you can talk yourself into getting up. Maybe you rehearse in your mind what's ahead, or remind yourself of something you want to do, or maybe you simply use your assertive self to tell your inert self to get moving. However you do it, you successfully make this first transition of the day from sleep to wakefulness because you can think about it and reason with yourself.

Children on the autism spectrum find transition very difficult. It's because transition triggers anxiety about what might happen next. This anxiety can override the ability to think and reason and act. It's because we get frightened that we get stuck. We all do! Staying in a stuck place is a way to protect ourselves from change or moving on. So in this chapter I'm going to tell you two stories that illustrate how children got stuck and how the group experience helped them to move on, develop and grow.

Learning to regulate feelings and behaviour when something is new

LAWRENCE AND THE VISITOR

Every so often we have a visitor in the Friendly Group. Over the years the visitors have included psychology students, teachers, therapists and psychologists. The appearance of someone new changes the dynamic of a group session and will always create tension. However a visitor also creates an opportunity for the children to develop their resilience around the uncertainty that change brings, and enhance their social skills with an unfamiliar adult. The children are always prepared for a visitor the week before such a visit, sharing discussion about how they feel about meeting someone new in the group.

One day Donna came for a session. She was a teacher from a local school and was planning to set up her own group. She wanted to have some understanding of how the groups work and to enhance her skills. As she already knew a child from one of the groups, we were careful to choose a group of children aged nine to eleven whom she had never met before, to maintain confidentiality and boundaries.

Marco was the first to arrive and was on the trampoline before I had had a chance to tell him that Donna was there. He looked momentarily shocked when he realised, but when I reminded him that Donna was the visitor we were expecting he waved at her and she waved back. Alfie came in next, and much to my surprise, greeted Donna when I introduced him. Normally he avoided others and averted eye contact, shuffling or sliding away to walk the perimeter of the garden space. Today, he gave an unexpectedly normal greeting and then went on his ritual circuit. My two colleagues continued supervising the children as I went to the gate to welcome each child as they arrived before introducing them to Donna, so that by the time we were ready to go inside, she had said hello to each of them. Lawrence made no acknowledgement of Donna and was the only one who walked past as if she was not there.

I went inside ahead of the others to sort out the cushions and saw Lawrence playing with the bricks in the inner room. He had made an elaborate tower and looked focused in his play. *"I playing these bricks,"* he announced in his halting style, indicating with his limited language that he was not going to join the others as they began to enter the group room. Lawrence was demonstrating through his actions what he had not yet learnt to articulate safely in words; that he felt unsure about leaving the security of his play with bricks and joining the group with a visitor present.

"I can see you have made a lovely tower there, Lawrence, and I know you like playing with the bricks. But it's time to join the circle now. You can leave it all there and carry on at choosing time," I said, realising that Lawrence was not going to budge.
"I staying here to play. I not coming in," said Lawrence emphatically as he continued to handle the bricks and without looking at me.
"I know it can be a worry when we have someone new in the group," I ventured.

In the last couple of weeks I had noticed that Lawrence had been struggling to engage; he was at the end of his final year of primary school and there were many transitions going on and being prepared for. After initially being very playful and engaged with the other children; such as creating *clapping* and *follow my leader* games on the trampoline and sharing his worries over a forthcoming sleepover at school, Lawrence had recently become much more withdrawn when we were doing the talking parts of the session. However, he always sat with the other children and they accepted him being quiet. The arrival of Donna was clearly too much for him.

I could have felt in a dilemma, torn between encouraging Lawrence to join us and formally starting the session with a welcome for Donna. The more I encouraged

Lawrence in, the more determined he was to stay where he was. Memories flooded back of the times, a year earlier, when Lawrence had not only refused to join in, but had also thrown cushions at me, stomped around the room and wailed like a baby, alarming some of the other children. What he was doing at that time was testing how much I could bear. The children saw that his behaviours didn't destroy or anger me, I could tolerate the disturbances in the sessions. It also showed I would be able to tolerate their disturbances too.

However, a year later, with Donna there, I could feel myself beginning to tense up. The relaxing start to the session in the garden had lulled me into a false sense of security that all would flow smoothly. Some visitors can look rather unsure, but Donna, wearing casual shorts and a beaming smile, looked so comfortable amongst the children, that the rest of them seemed to accept her presence straight away. I inwardly reminded myself that I didn't need to 'look after' Donna and that what was happening with Lawrence was an important communication about difficulties with transition, and needed a response.

The circle was formed and we all sat down. One of the double doors was still open to the room from where Lawrence was resolutely refusing to budge. His body shape could be seen through the frosted glass of the closed half. His blurred figure was holding the tension.

> *"Where's Lawrence?"* asked Andrew, who felt great discomfort if there were any changes and was extremely sensitive.
> *"He is choosing to stay in the other room at the moment,"* I answered.
> *"But we all need to be together for the stone and we have a visitor as well,"* persisted Andrew.
> *"I agree that we are normally all together in the same room. However Lawrence doesn't feel able to join the group right now,"* I added, noticing

from the corner of my eye, that Lawrence had stopped what he was doing and was listening very carefully to every word.

"I wonder how you feel about that and I wonder what we can do about it," I continued as the children sat watching and listening to me.

The presence of a stranger had heightened the emotional atmosphere to one of tense expectation. Would anyone be able to say what needed to be said? There was Lawrence, waiting in the wings, not knowing what to do with his anxiety and not knowing what to say. The margins can be a frightening place to be; there is an inner conflict about whether to join or not to join in and the discomfort of the 'stuck' place you find yourself in when you have taken the position of withdrawal.

In the silence that followed, Lawrence's silence spoke to everyone in the group. Each of the children recognised that inner conflict and those feelings of uncertainty in themselves. They 'knew' Lawrence's experience even if they didn't know how Lawrence was feeling right then. However, they had a feel for what he was feeling. If these feelings were not expressed or spoken about in the group, Lawrence would be trapped in his isolation, because he was holding that role for all of them. I wondered if the group was mature enough for any of the children to speak up.

Donna, sitting opposite me, caught my eye with a look of concern. She had taken on the 'teacher' response and was seeing the situation as my authority being challenged in front of a stranger. Then she looked across at the small boy sitting to my left, who was now speaking in a loud and clear voice.

"I remember when Lawrence stayed in the other room before," said Tim.
"Yes, I remember it too," agreed Marco who was sitting rather stiffly, *"and I think we should let him play until he is ready to come and join us."*
"Yes! I think we should let Lawrence play," added Tim with a releasing sigh

in his voice. Marco's posture also softened as his suggestion was affirmed. Lawrence had got nearer to the doorway now.

"That is really kind of you both, Marco and Tim. You are being very understanding about Lawrence not wanting to come in. You understand it is difficult for him today because we have a visitor," I said, scanning the whole group. I then went on to address Donna, so that all the children could hear.

"Donna! In the Friendly Group, we're kind to one another by considering others' feelings. You can see it happening today. It's sometimes difficult to join the group when there is someone new here. It can feel safer to stay in the other room. Sometimes it's difficult to share our feelings and ideas especially in front of someone we don't know. It's best when we can all sit in the circle together, but Tim and Marco have shown that they understand how Lawrence is feeling. And they are saying that it's okay to be a little different today. After all, it's different to have you visiting us as well."

I hoped my words would explain further what was happening and to help the children to be able to think about the situation. After a short pause in which a little bit of relaxed wriggling took place, I continued.

"I wonder what the rest of you think? Are you happy for Lawrence to stay in the other room?"

Hearing his name, Lawrence withdrew again, seeking refuge in a contained space. He reminded me of a tortoise with the frame of the door being like the rim of his shell. There was a chorus of assent and the session began. First of all I opened the other door so Lawrence was visible and no longer able to hide behind the frosted glass. He didn't protest but by remaining where he was he could regulate his distance and level of stimulation. He still fiddled with the bricks, but I could see that he was listening to what was being said and watching what was going on. His threshold place was neither threatening for him nor for the other children and it allowed him to manage his anxiety.

> *"This is Lawrence's cushion,"* I said, pointing to the cushion immediately to my right and in front of the wide doorway, *"so we know when it is Lawrence's turn."*
> *"Today, as we have Donna visiting us, I am going to suggest that we go round the circle with each of you introducing yourselves and saying what you like about the Friendly Group,"* I said, to start the group talking.
> *"I like the Friendly Group because we do exciting adventures when we make up the story together,"* was the first offering.
> *"I like the trampoline,"* was another.

We went round the whole group. Lawrence was the last to speak and came to the threshold of the doorway, standing just behind his cushion. *"I like the Friendly Group because I like playing with my friends."*

In that sentence Lawrence was able to put into in words that he didn't feel separate, even though he physically was in that moment; he felt a part of the group. He had found a way to put thoughts into speech rather than action. Even though he was still slightly on the edge, when talking on the threshold, he had managed to move in from the margins to the centre and become an integral member of the group. The group had 'contained' his need to be separate but close, for the moment. On the edge, but still an accepted and connected part of the whole. This is the experience that these children so badly need - rather than feeling so anxious they split away altogether.

Learning to regulate feelings and behaviour when you're feeling upset

KEITH'S STORY: STUCK IN THE CAR

It was pouring with rain and we had gathered in the group room but we were still waiting for Keith (12). This well-established group of mainly teenagers was happy to chat, enjoying easy and lighthearted banter with each other. Just as I was about to suggest we should make a start, Keith's mother Esther appeared at the door. She stepped inside, dripping wet and apologised about being on her own. Then she poured out her story, words tumbling out with great urgency and a tone of voice that betrayed helplessness and desperation. Keith had got his exam results and they were not as good as he had hoped. He was told he would have to retake Maths and Biology. He was devastated and in anger had thrown his phone, which had smashed and broken. Now he refused to get out of the car.

Forgetting to put on a coat, I followed Esther to the car that was parked on the road nearby. Keith had climbed into the back seat, obscured by black tinted windows and had locked the door. Luckily, the front passenger door was wide open and I was able to put my head in. *"Hello Keith,"* I said quietly.

Keith hid behind his hood and rocked and whimpered. I made reassuring noises and he got as far as unlocking the door. Then he opened it. Esther had held back up to this point, but now she was by my side.

> *"I can understand if it's difficult for you to come in the group today, but Gary was looking forward to seeing you. Maybe if you don't want to leave the car, Gary could at least come to you and say a quick hello and goodbye?"*

Keith said nothing. He was crying with tears rolling down his cheeks. I returned to the group room, now rather wet from the rain. When I explained the problem and asked if Gary (13) could come out, the others wanted to come too, but it was decided that the rest of the group and the other adults should stay behind. Maybe if Gary was on his own, Keith might feel more confident to come and join the rest of us.

Gary put on his raincoat and followed me to the car. I stood back as he huddled at the open rear door. Keith was still crying. Esther had walked down the road. She too was crying, her tears joining the raindrops dripping from the hood of her raincoat. I went up to her.

> *"I just want Keith to know that he is safe with these friends here and that he can trust them,"* she mumbled.
> *"It will be OK,"* I said and gave her a reassuring hug, which she welcomed more than my words.

I returned to the car. Keith was not going to budge. Gary looked at me with regret in his eyes before turning back to Keith and saying, *"I hope you feel better soon, Keith."* The two of us then went back to the group room, rather wet and feeling a bit flat. I could tell that Gary felt disappointed like me, and shared this in the group. Gary was able to say the same.

> *"Keith will have heard what you said, Gary,"* began my colleague Claire, *"And this will have helped him even if it was just too difficult to come in today."*
> *"I know how Keith feels,"* said Annie (14). *"It's really difficult to go in somewhere once you've said you won't."*

This opened up a conversation with the whole group about these stuck feelings. Keith may not have been physically present, but his presence was felt nonetheless. We were just about to start the formal *Circle Time with the stone* (albeit 15 minutes late), when Keith unexpectedly walked in. The delight and love in that room was palpable as the group discreetly made space for him to sit down. I briefly acknowledged Keith's arrival by saying we had only just started, but said no more, so that he would not be overwhelmed. Keith had taken a brave step in coming in. When Gary held the stone, he turned to Keith and said, *"I'm glad you have come in Keith."*

Each person had their turn and when it came to Keith's turn, he held the stone, looking down at it. I reminded him that he didn't have to say anything right then and he looked up and glanced at me to acknowledge this before passing the stone on. The session continued. Keith was quiet but visibly relaxed as the session proceeded in the normal way and no unusual demands or expectations were made of him. By the time it came to *choosing time* the group naturally broke up into small sub-groups. Two of them decided to move into the inner room and play the piano together. Another chose to look at a book. Two others talked to Claire. And Keith could be seen laughing with Gary and Annie as if there had been no difficulty whatsoever only half an hour before.

When we reconvened at the end and the youngsters took turns to share their special moments of the session, this is what Annie said to the whole group.

> *"I don't want to embarrass you Keith, but my special moment was when you came in today. I know that feeling when you've said you won't go somewhere and it's very hard to then do it."*

Up to that time, Annie had treated the group as if it was a youth club. She'd said she liked to come and meet the others and to have some fun, but she'd been unable to share her feelings. On this day, Keith's difficulty had not only given her an opportunity to connect with him as well as with the whole group, but also to be able to express and reflect on her feelings.

When it was Keith's turn to speak, I expected the usual mumbles or maybe no comment at all. Keith had always been a very reticent member of the group and when he did speak it barely came out as a whisper, even when he had enjoyed himself. The act of talking out loud in front of a group was extremely stressful for him. Today was different: his voice was clear and strong.

> *"My best moment of today was chatting and having a laugh with Gary and Annie, just now ... it was brilliant!"*

The session came to a close and I went out ahead of the youngsters to greet their parents. By this time, the rain had stopped and I was met with a row of expectant faces standing on the paved area outside. Esther had managed to get down to the café and join the other parents. She had also told them about Keith's outburst, so now it was all the parents who were wondering how it all had gone. The shared delight that Keith had been OK brought the group of parents closer together that day.

Keith continued to be a quiet member of the group, but he was able to share his feelings and began to give others' support. More importantly he became more confident at home and at school. The exam retakes went well and Keith went on to do well at school, eventually achieving success at university.

> **THINGS TO THINK ABOUT**
>
> Although we all feel anxious and overwhelmed at times, especially when we are feeling pressurised or facing something new, we know that we have to somehow manage these feelings so we can cope and keep going. We develop coping strategies to regulate our emotions and calm ourselves down.
>
> The trouble is that highly sensitive children or children on the autism spectrum take much longer to develop these strategies. It's because their fright response is triggered very quickly, so it takes much less stimuli to arouse, distress and overwhelm them. The simple transition of moving from one thing to another can trigger enough anxiety to stop them in their tracks. Whether you're a parent or a professional, these behaviours can be frustrating and perplexing, so I hope the two stories in this chapter, which describe how children have helped each other, will help you.

CHAPTER 15

The Café Group

In Chapter 3 I've described how important I feel it is for parents to become involved in the Friendly Group. One of the ways I help parents with this is to provide an evening session once a term, which is facilitated by me and another colleague. The session lasts for one and a half hours. We sit in a circle and share refreshments. One purpose of the session is to be able to give parents some feedback as to how their children are getting on. Another purpose is to offer the parents a safe space (a bit like the children have) to share their worries and hopes. Great strength can be gained from finding you are not alone; there are others who are going through the same experiences as you.

Before the parents' sessions my colleagues and I establish with the children what they would like us to share with their parents. The teenagers in particular need reassurance that we will not break any trust in confidentiality. However, the younger children usually like us to share their experiences with their parents. Whilst I do still share some of the children's stories about what has happened in the group (because the parents enjoy them) my present emphasis is more about creating opportunities for parents to talk about their own feelings; their hopes and uncertainties, their worries and delights. They have the opportunity to find their own voices, are witness to each others' struggles and reach out to support one another, just as the children do on a Saturday morning. Indeed I have noticed a strong relationship between the children's ability to engage in the group process (whatever level of social skill they have) and the parents' commitment to coming to the evening sessions as well as meeting up with each other at the café on Saturdays.

If you are a parent reading this, you may be able to identify with some of the following stories and feelings I am going to tell. If you're a professional, perhaps it will give you more insight into how parents of the children and young people described in this book feel and think in relation to their children, their families and the outside world.

At the beginning of the story below (told during an evening parents' session), Kurt refers to his experience of informally joining other parents for coffee on a Saturday morning, while the children are taking part in the group. Later in the chapter I will describe how valuable these informal get-togethers are. The parents and I have nicknamed that regular coming together the 'Café Group'.

One Thursday evening parents' session

> *"Our Saturday morning get-togethers at the café are the highlight of my week!"* announced Kurt, one of the relatively new fathers at the evening parents' session. He then realised what he had said and looked momentarily embarrassed.
>
> *"How sad is that! I bet it makes you wonder what my social life is like,"* he continued as his wife Juliet looked on, smiling beside him.

It was only about 15 minutes earlier, when making coffee and tea for the parents in the next room, that I could hear loud chatting and laughter. It had sounded like a party was going on. I could hear in the tone of that laughter that this was a well-established group of people who had bonded with one another. However, it seemed that Kurt's comment, in front of me and one of my colleagues, might have slightly unsettled the others. Maybe he had exposed something private about the group? Maybe the group members were unconsciously wondering what my colleague and I would think of them? However, this slightly awkward tension was held for only seconds and then broken.

"I know what you mean," added Naomi and the others quietly sighed and then visibly leaned forward. *"It is so good to be able to talk with other people who understand. I have lots of friends and they're very supportive. They know about my son's problems, but I know that really they get bored when I keep telling them about him. They don't know what it's like. But on a Saturday when we get together I know I can relax and you will listen. And what is more, I know that you understand and that is such a relief."*

"I agree with both of you," said Jenny, a mother who was usually rather reserved and quiet. *"What I like so much is the way we can laugh about the children. They do such strange things at times but some of these things are really funny. I know that other people would think we were being cruel, but we're not. If you can't laugh sometimes, you just cry and feel afraid and it all gets too much."*

"Yes! It's great to discover that your child is doing exactly the same as someone else's. You don't feel so alone," said Clive.

The atmosphere became charged with urgency to express feelings of appreciation, gratitude and relatedness.

"I really appreciated the way you all supported me that day I was so upset when Arthur was being bullied in school. I didn't feel embarrassed about

crying and the pent-up tension I had felt for ages just went. Things seemed to get better after that and I always put it down to you guys, I don't know why!" continued Donna.

Memories of times when they had helped one another began to be shared. Groups strengthen when the members are able to acknowledge and recognise their shared history; it reinforces the feelings of connection and with it, wellbeing. This parents' session was giving this group of people a place to be able to say openly and in front of one another, *"We are a group; this group is important and means something to me"*.

"What I really like about the group is the way when we get together I feel normal," blurted out Louise, who had only recently joined the group.

Everyone laughed because they knew exactly what she meant. However, Louise continued with her train of thought.

"So often, when I go out, I feel I have to explain myself because Elizabeth's behaviour can be so bad and I know people are judging me. Or when I go out with friends on my own, I can tell that my friends are being 'extra nice' because they know they are 'giving me a break'. The trouble is it makes me feel different. They're not exactly giving me sympathy, but I feel like some sad soul. I know that they mean well but it makes me wonder if I'm normal. On Saturdays I don't even have to think like that! We're all in it together somehow, even though our children are so very different."

"And we are all so different too!" added Louise's husband Denis. *"That's what makes it interesting. We find out things about each other and about*

other useful things like where you got that good deal on your car, Clive. I like the fact we don't just talk about the children. I think we can just relax because we all know our children are safe."

Denis had touched on a theme which, since starting the Friendly Group, has come up in all the parents' evening sessions. We are told time and time again by the parents that because they feel their children are safe and happy for the hour, it enables them to relax. They can leave their children without that niggling anxiety that they might be telephoned to say that he or she is having a 'meltdown' and could they come and fetch them. They are confident that when they do pick up their children at the end of the session, they won't be faced with a backlash of anger or tears that so often greets them after some time away from the routine and safety of home. What the parents do not necessarily realise is that it is their confidence in the Friendly Group that contributes to the very success of it.

I raised this at a parents' session quite recently. It is easy for the parents to become so enchanted by their child's happiness and progress, that they attribute this all to me and my colleagues. They are in danger of treating me and my colleagues with a kind of admiring reverence, which is preventing them from understanding what is really happening and the role they play within that.

"I don't understand what you do!" we are often told, *"But it's a kind of magic! I've never seen my child so happy and so normal as when he comes here. I usually have to drag him out of the house to go anywhere but on a Saturday morning he gets up first and is telling me to hurry up!"*

It is a well-known dynamic in group therapy that the leader will be initially idealised and put on a pedestal. However, there is no room to manoeuvre in that fixed position, so the necessary and inevitable 'knocking down' from the pedestal is also part of that dynamic. If you have ever been part of a group yourself, where you have felt inspired by the leader, you will probably recognise there is a kind of longing to be like that 'magical' person. However, with time you will probably have felt some disillusionment when you felt the leader has in some way let you down or maybe you have felt you have let the leader down. We all have to go through this period of disillusionment with ourselves and others to get to the 'middle ground' and be able to grow and develop. It's like the infant who sees a mother as doing no wrong, followed by the disillusionment of adolescence and finally the integration of adulthood. I continue to explain about the group:

> *"It is not so much about what we 'do' as about the 'quality of the experience' that the children are having when they are here. We're not necessarily setting up planned activities to occupy them, or to teach them specific skills. What we are doing is providing a predictable and regular framework, which create opportunities for your children to simply 'be themselves' and reflect on who they are and how they feel about it."*

At this point I show them the framework (described in Chapter 4).

> *"We don't see your child's diagnosed pathology,"* is how I usually start. *"We look for the person inside. We see the longings, the anxieties, the mischievousness, the sensitivities, the enthusiasms and the confusions that are in all of them. I put myself in their shoes and wonder what it must be like to go to an unfamiliar place for the first time, not knowing what the 'social rules' are or whether the people will make me feel at ease or awkward. I think about my own childhood and adolescent longings and anxieties and*

the deep desire to feel a part of something without shame, awkwardness or embarrassment. We understand that being with other people is stressful. We understand that some children desperately want to make relationships, whilst others are more interested in objects, stories and their own fantasy worlds. We want to get to know your child's personality so that we can be sensitive to the way we speak to them or behave with them, so they'll feel at ease with themselves."

When I start to talk in this way, I notice that the parents can begin to get in touch with their own experiences as well. As human beings, we all share in the same struggle for meaning and for a sense of place and belonging. When we know we can trust a person, a group or a situation, we can relax. When we feel that someone else cares, it touches our souls. We may not realise it at the time but this helps us to reflect on and process our anxieties or troubles. We then discover that we feel a lot better. We begin to trust that we can cope and things will be OK. We develop our self-confidence.

As the parents begin to trust that their children will be safe and happy at the Friendly Group, they are unconsciously giving these confident energies to their children. At a deep level, which goes beyond any rational thinking, the children pick up on their parents' trust in them and they begin to trust themselves. The parents see that their children are happy in the group and they are happy. The children see that their parents are happy about them coming to the group and *they* are happy. Little by little, the children and their parents find themselves enjoying other experiences and places. The trip to the cinema or the restaurant becomes fun rather than stressful. The forthcoming holiday becomes something to be eagerly anticipated rather than dreaded. The play date is arranged and turns out to be a success. These social and family experiences grow, not because of anything that I and my colleagues may have done, *but because the parents and their children are growing more confident in each others' company*. They are becoming more sensitively responsive and tuned into the whole spectrum of emotions associated with love, rather than stuck with the emotions associated with fear. They are building the foundations for securely attached relationships.

A FATHER'S FIRST EXPERIENCE OF AN EVENING PARENTS' SESSION

Although most of the fathers take their turn in bringing their children on a Saturday, this isn't always the case. So it was with Rick's father. Rick's mother, Geraldine, had told me that her husband was 'unsure' about the Friendly Group and I would probably never meet him. I was told that he was an academically bright man and brilliant at his work but had always found socialising difficult. He could see no reason why his son needed to come to the group; his son was bright like him and seemed fine to him. Geraldine however, witnessed the many family arguments as her husband failed to pick up the social cues with their children. Rick *was* similar to his father and was having difficulties making successful peer relationships in school. Rick desperately wanted to have friends and had been a keen member of the Friendly Group for about two years. He saw the value of the group and was beginning to have some social success at school. His mother, Geraldine, always brought him on a Saturday. She herself was a keen member of the Café Group, and she always came to the parents' sessions. Then one evening, about ten minutes before a parents' session was due to start, the phone rang.

> *"Hello Anita! It's Geraldine here. I'm sorry but I can't make it to the parents' session tonight as I've only just got back home from work and I'm tired and I haven't eaten. I wouldn't be able to make it either as it takes about half an hour to get over to you. I rang Milo earlier on my mobile and told him he had to come tonight in my place. I hope he makes it okay.*

He left before I got back," said Geraldine in rather a breathless voice.

I wondered what Milo would be like, how the evening would go. Geraldine had painted a picture that led me to believe that he was rather uncertain about the group. I wanted to discuss how the recent negativity of one of the children had been unsettling for the other children in the group and wondered how he might respond to such a discussion. My thoughts were making me feel a little anxious. However, I was soon taken out of my reverie because minutes later the doorbell rang, and an unfamiliar and gentle faced man at the door was asking if I was Anita and telling me he was Milo, Rick's father. I welcomed him in and told him he was the first to arrive and that it was good to meet him. I also said that I was delighted that he was able to join us for the evening. Milo followed me into the group room with a grin of embarrassment on his face and chose to sit on a chair on the far side of the room.

I immediately warmed towards Milo. I could see he was nervous and wanted to put him at his ease. I first introduced him to my colleague, Jo, then I reassured him that Geraldine had already telephoned and so I knew he was coming. This seemed to please him and he looked relieved to hear this news. Six of the eight children's parents came that night; three couples, Milo and two mothers.

On this occasion it was the first evening session for another father, Geoffrey and a couple, Niall and Bridget. The couple had already 'joined' the Café Group, but Geoffrey, like Milo, had not been to the café. He had, however, brought his daughter on a Saturday, from time to time, and had come this evening with his wife. The third couple had only been once before to a parents' session. The remaining three mothers had been to several evening sessions.

I was curious to see how the evening would go and how the group would work together. As it turned out, the shy Milo led the way when it was his turn to introduce himself to the group. We had been passing the stone around. The parents, like the children on their first Saturday, were invited to hold the stone and say something about themselves. Everyone else would listen without interrupting. One by one they took their turn until finally Milo had the stone in his hands.

> *"My name is Milo and my 11-year-old son, Rick attends this group. I've never been here before so I don't know any of you. I've been sent by my wife Geraldine this evening. I didn't even know I was coming until an hour ago. I had to leave my teenage daughter in charge at home till Geraldine got back from work. I'm rather nervous about being here this evening. You see, I'm like the children who come on Saturday. I've recently found out that I have Asperger's Syndrome. I didn't know I had the syndrome when I was a child. I just knew I was different and I didn't like to mix with people. Well, I have to say it's really difficult for me tonight. It's a nightmare for me to come into a room like this with people I've never met before."* Milo spoke in a steady voice and with a steadily flushing face.

You could have heard a pin drop. He had touched a collective nerve. He had openly and honestly expressed his feelings and opened the gateway for others to do the same. Instead of the focus being on how they were feeling about their children, the group began talking about themselves.

> *"I can understand that it must be very difficult for you,"* I acknowledged.
> *"I wonder if anyone else has anything to say or feels in any way like Milo."*

In acknowledging what Milo had said, I was focusing on the group process, the here-and-now feelings about what was happening right then.

"Well I would like to add to what Milo has said," began Niall. Whenever he picked up his son on a Saturday, Niall had always presented himself as either rather a 'joker' or seemed awkwardly silent. His tone was quite different now; there was gravitas about it. *"I am really glad you said what you did about having Asperger's."*

"Normally I don't like to say anything, but I think I have got Asperger's Syndrome as well. My wife here thinks so!" and Niall looked at his wife, sitting still beside him.

"I find it very difficult going into social situations like you, Milo. You are brave to come here on your own," he went on. *"At least I have Bridget with me tonight. I didn't know what to expect and when I came in and saw the circle of chairs it made me a bit worried that I might have to talk. And here I am talking! But what I wanted to say was that I think my son's problems are because of me and I feel really bad about it. When the school express their concerns about him and describe what he is like, I think 'That sounds like me at his age!' I feel that I need help as much as my son."*

"Yes! I know what you mean," agreed Milo, *"but I don't usually admit it, especially not to Geraldine my wife! I know she finds me difficult at times and I just cover it up by pretending I haven't heard or by not agreeing with what she says. I can't bear to think that my son has problems that have been caused by me,"* said Milo with a fair bit of emotion in his rising voice and reddening face.

This was when Esther stepped in with her comments. Esther, with her long blond hair and fine features, nearly always wore a serious expression on her face. She worried all the time about her son's physical and mental health problems, her parenting skills and her social skills. Whilst desperately wanting to fit in to the Café Group and getting a lot of support from it at times, she often felt overwhelmed on the Saturday morning at the prospect of being with others and would excuse herself by taking her dog for a walk or going shopping instead. Having said very little earlier, when she had the stone in her hands, she now began to speak,

> *"I know exactly what you mean. I am always blaming myself for my son's problems. Not just Keith who comes to the Friendly group, but my daughter as well. She has lots of anxieties like me too. That's the main trouble, I have so many anxieties and phobias and I feel I am passing them on. One of the problems I have with Keith is that he won't go on public transport and he's 14. He just can't cope with it. I can understand him but I can't cope with his problem."*
>
> *"I have exactly the same trouble with Max,"* said Bridget, Niall's wife, now eager to join in the discussion.
>
> *"I drive seventy eight miles a day to and from my son's school because he won't go in the school taxi and he's almost the same age as your son,"* explained Bridget, looking over to Esther.

There was a feeling of understanding rippling around the room. No-one was giving unwanted advice. No-one was looking for sympathy. This is what they live with and it was just a relief to be able to describe it as it is without anyone interrupting with unwelcome solutions. After all, this group of parents and many others have been trying to solve these kinds of problems for years.

As the evening developed, my colleague Jo and I described some of the things we had been doing with the children. We mentioned that they can draw pictures while creating their story together. At this point Bridget interrupted.

"Does Max do any drawing?" she asked, but before Jo could give an answer, she continued, *"Well, I bet he doesn't. He is very sensitive to pencils."*

"Well, it is happening," said Jo, *"I can't say that I've noticed what he is using to do his drawings. It could well be a felt pen or ball point pen because we have those as well as pencils."*

"I'm surprised he isn't making a fuss about the other children using pencils," added Bridget, *"especially as the room is small and the children are quite close to one another."*

"This is really interesting Bridget," adds Jo, *"Because Max has never said anything about pencils. He has joined in and has not seemed worried in any way about them. Somehow he is managing to cope. Although he is new to the group he has actually opened up and expressed other worries and seems relaxed and open with everyone."*

"I agree with your last comments," added Bridget. *"That is why Niall and I were so interested in coming this evening. Max has never wanted to join any group before and he's 12. He says he wants to make friends, but when we have tried with other things it all seems to go wrong."*

It was at this point that one of the other parents spoke up and told the group that her son had also had a 'thing' about pencils, but was OK with it now. She had thought he was the only child who had ever had a problem with pencils.

"Well, Max was certainly the only one in his school at one time," continued Bridget, *"I had a terrible battle with them. It was when he was at primary school and they just wouldn't accept that he has a real sensory problem. We were told that it was their Maths policy for the children to use a pencil right up to the end of Year 6. Although Max was only nine or ten at the time, I*

suggested that he should write to his class teacher and try to explain his problems to her himself. He said he would and he ended up writing a much longer letter than we or he expected. He described how it gave him pains up his leg and his side and all sorts of other things too. When his teacher read the letter she burst into tears and was much more sympathetic after that."

The group were clearly fascinated by Bridget's story. They could relate to what she had said and began to share the various sensory issues of their own children. However, it was Esther who told us her own story.

"I think I should explain that I think I have Asperger's Syndrome too," she began, *"I can identify with Max's problem over the pencils. The worst thing is that people just don't believe you and they often torment you with it as well. I have never said anything to you before, but I am really oversensitive about the feel of knitted wool,"* she said, rubbing her hands.

It looked as if she was stroking her smooth black trousers, but she was actually just skimming the surface of them. I could see she was having trouble even speaking about wool, but now she had started talking she got into the flow and couldn't stop. The group waited in transfixed silence.

"I just hate the feel of it," she said with a grimace on her face, *"I can't begin to describe the horrid sensations I get if I touch a knitted wool jumper or dress. The worst thing is that I can't bear it if I see other people touching anything made of wool; it's like I'm touching it myself. And if I mention it to any adults, do you know what they immediately do? They stroke their own woollen clothing and come close to me to do it. They think they're making*

a joke but it's no joke to me. And I feel so foolish about it too. I can't think what children go through who have sensitivities towards things. Children, and especially teenagers, can be so cruel to one another. I think this is another thing that makes me so worried about my children. I am always afraid they are going to get bullied and teased for their differences."

This opened up the floodgates for talking about their children's experiences of being bullied. Francis's parents, Andrea and Leon, began talking about their concerns. They described how their son had been bullied at school; how he found it very difficult to make friends, taking on the role of the clown or 'buying' friendships through gifts of sweets and so on. They were also concerned about his negativity towards most things in his life, especially when trying new things. He was currently negative about the Friendly Group and had told his parents he didn't want to continue. They were unsure as to whether he should continue or not.

"I know exactly what you are talking about," said Felicity. Everyone looked in Felicity's direction. She had been quiet up to that point. Felicity also had a 12-year-old son, but unlike 13-year-old Francis, who had only recently started in the group, Danny started when he was 10 and enjoyed coming.

"And I know exactly how you feel," she continued *"I am always worrying but my husband Darren, is much more positive than me and has always insisted that Danny should try new things. He dragged him to a football match once and I was worried that the crowds would be 'too much' for him. But do you know each time he does something new, Danny discovers he enjoys himself! He actually thanked us for taking him to the football match and asked to go again. But even though he keeps on having positive new experiences, he's still reluctant to try the next 'new' thing. We carry on doing*

it though. One day we hope he will begin to embrace the 'new' and not be so frightened of it. He was ill last year and had so much to go through. That seems to have made him stronger actually."

Frank and open exchanges about feelings and experiences lead to relationships being made between parents, expanding the narrow worlds that some of them find themselves inhabiting. Greater possibilities open up and can be thought about and tried. Many parents believe that a diagnosis of autism means that their children can't learn about social norms and empathy, but this really isn't the case. They can learn, and they do develop naturally.

The Café Group and how it began

There is also another rather potent agent at work on a Saturday morning. It is not just that the children come to the Friendly Group and the parents can see they are happy. As I have already said at the beginning of this chapter, the parents join one another informally for a coffee in a local café, while their children are attending the group. I call this the 'Café Group'. When I started the Friendly Group eighteen years ago, one or two of the parents, who had driven a long way to get to the group, asked if there was somewhere nearby where they could get a cup of coffee or tea. As the local pub wasn't open that early in the morning, I directed them to a local café. I didn't think much about it.

Over time more and more parents began to meet together at the café. I discovered they were teaming up and giving each other lifts to avoid all taking cars. They began to wait for one another outside the gate before setting off. They would let each other know if they were going to miss a week or were going to be a bit late. At the café they shared bacon sandwiches, cakes, coffee, hot chocolate and tea. Younger siblings sometimes went along as well, playing on the little trampoline there.

A developing friendliness among the parents began to emerge. It was as if they could let out their joint breaths at the café for an hour each week, relieved to have found others sharing similar experiences to themselves. Most of all they were developing as a group in their own right, so by the time they came for the scheduled evening parents' session with us they knew one another quite well. There was no need for introductions, except that they took it upon themselves to welcome the occasional parent who, for whatever reason, hadn't met up at the café. The parents' familiarity with each other meant that instead of meeting a collection of individuals I was now facilitating a well-established group in its own right.

So why is the Café Group itself so important? It's not come about by accident. Nowadays we always encourage new parents to join the others at the café while their children are attending the group if they can. I acknowledge that they might prefer to do something else during that piece of free time, but that it is worth at least trying once. In my experience, parents enjoy meeting others in the same situations as themselves.

Part of the philosophy of the Friendly Group is that the children develop better if their parents are also engaged. There is a parallel process between the Friendly Group and the Café Group. The parents experience for themselves the benefits of being in a group. In the same way as the Friendly Group creates a safe place for the children, the café provides a safe place for the parents. It is a neutral place where the 'old hander' parents can be hospitable to the newly joined parents. They can sit around a table and talk to one another ... or not. Sometimes at the parents' evening sessions the group has chuckled with the occasional father (never the mothers, I have noticed) who has told us that at the café, he chooses to read his newspaper or look at his phone at the adjacent table rather than join in the conversation! It reminds me of the children who have occasionally sat behind the curtain or lain down under the bookshelf. They still want to be with the group but have preserved their own privacy when the social conversation has felt like 'too much'.

At one evening session, the parents requested that I create a list of their contact details to share with each other. I wondered if this particular group possibly felt that they needed to have my permission to get to know one another outside the Friendly Group. One of the mothers laughed at herself and admitted that the list would be a great help to her because just as her son still didn't know the names of the other children, neither could she remember the names of the other parents even though she knew a lot about them!

By contrast other groups have taken the initiative themselves, not only to exchange contact details but to arrange their own group get-togethers. There have been other groups of parents who have met up for picnics or to taken their children for an activity such as bowling. Individual friendships between parents and children have also flourished over the years and the occasional teenage romance has blossomed and faded as well.

Children can learn

Parents are involved in the Friendly Group in several different ways. They meet us before we meet their children and in some cases they come for ongoing individual counselling for themselves alongside the work we are doing with their children. Some families come for family counselling sessions during the gaps between group blocks of sessions. All the parents are invited to attend the once-a-term evening parents' sessions. Most parents become informal members of the peer group of parents, the Café Group, described above.

This variety of support enhances not only parental confidence, but facilitates children's learning. Time and time again, I hear comments like, *"I didn't think he could do that, because he's autistic,"* or *"I felt we couldn't change a routine because of all the meltdowns,"* or *"I thought she would never make friends because she's autistic,"* or *"I didn't know children with Asperger's could understand feelings,"* or *"I never thought my child could learn social stuff."*

Autism Spectrum Disorder is a developmental disorder, but that child will still develop and can learn. A child on the autism spectrum may grow up thinking, sensing and interpreting information in a different way than most other children, but it would be doing these children a disservice if we believed they could not develop and learn to fit in and be happy with themselves.

All children can learn and all children on the autism spectrum can learn. They need trust, understanding, patience, confidence and consistency from the adults who care and educate them to be able to develop. Parents can feel very lost and isolated. Parents can feel overwhelmed by the huge amounts of information about autism these days. Parents can lose sight of children's abilities, lost in the forest of difficulties that their children face.

However, when parents get together and make relationships where they can freely share their feelings, they can become less stuck and in turn this helps the children in their learning. If you are a parent of a child who is struggling in one way or another, you will feel supported and your child will benefit if you are able to join a support group.

THINGS TO THINK ABOUT

For parents, having the opportunity to talk openly with other parents in a similar position is very empowering and supportive. The general themes which tend to come up range from concerns such as bullying in school and difficult behaviours at home to getting on with homework and coming off the computer (or rather, not wanting to come off the computer). However the bigger 'life' questions about how their children will cope as adults, are also often talked about In this chapter I have also illustrated how seemingly 'small things' to most children, like the sound of a pencil, can be disturbing, and are actually 'big things' to autistic children.

The National Autistic Society is a charitable organisation set up to support parents with children on the autism spectrum and has regional branches, where there are local parent groups. I recommend you try one of these if you are a parent and have a child whom you feel may have an Autism Spectrum Disorder or who has already been diagnosed.

If you are a professional who wants to run a group for parents, you will be offering something very positive and inclusive to people who often feel isolated. I hope that this chapter gives some insight into how to facilitate such a group. I would also recommend that you receive professional supervision (mentoring support) from a peer group or on an individual basis. You would need to either search what is available through your professional body or if you are working for a local authority, you could find out what is available locally or even set up a supervision group yourself.

CHAPTER 16

Cancer calls: Christopher's story

January

As Christopher hobbled outside at the end of one of the sessions, carefully placing his crutches step by step along the snowy path and reluctant to leave the group, his mother's voice could be heard calling, *"Come on! Hurry up! We've got to get going."*

And unobserved, except by me, Christopher paused and, as he lent on his left crutch for support, he lifted his right crutch a little above the ground. Then with great care and precision and using the crutch like a large crayon, he drew a picture of a smiley face in the pristine snow on the grassy bank by the path. Without any comment he simply re-hooked the crutch in his arm, hobbled towards his mother and headed out of the gate.

Christopher had left his mark. He had communicated something important and he knew I had received that communication. The Friendly Group had offered some healing that day for his hurting body and his anxious soul.

18 months earlier

Christopher (10) was typical of many children who have been a part of the Friendly Group over the years. An intelligent and creative boy, who loved stories and enjoyed talking to both adults and children, he nevertheless had found it difficult to sustain lasting relationships with his peer group. He had been diagnosed with Asperger's Syndrome when he was about six or seven years old, but his difficulties were subtle and caught both him and his family unawares. At that time, Christopher had a tendency to take things literally and more importantly, he misunderstood the playful intentions of other children and often interpreted their comments as mean and unkind. He was convinced that children were bullying him. His reactions would alienate him from others and he felt left out.

Christopher also had a great sense of 'justice' and if he saw someone doing something that he thought was 'wrong' (either breaking a rule or saying something unkind to someone else) he would tell the teacher. He was viewed by his peers as a snitch or telltale. He resented both this and the children whom he felt had isolated him. It's normal for all children to feel left out and resentful at times, but learning to survive and get over these 'fallings out' is part of the skill of developing successful social relationships. The trouble is that many children on the autism spectrum hold onto negative experiences and find it difficult to let go. So resentments can build up over years, gnawing away and interfering with the normal development of learning to play and laugh with others.

Christopher wanted to make friends and to be accepted by others and the way he did this was by copying what his peers said or did. Indeed Christopher often made clumsy attempts at jokes. He understood that humour is part of making friends, but his jokes often came out wrong; they were either laboured or not didn't quite hit the right spot. Indeed, what he said could be hurtful at times. He didn't realise this at first, but as his self-awareness grew, so did his self-consciousness about his social awkwardness and with it, his anxiety. He began to worry about whether he was saying the 'right thing' or not.

These worries about *'never being good enough'* spilled out into all aspects of his life and were affecting his schoolwork and his relationships within his family. Although he had a vivid imagination, he was unable to write stories and he got stuck when doing his English homework. His defences were up even at home with his younger siblings, where he was often confrontational with them in his attempt to take control in the games. He would find it hard to back down, wanting his own way. His parents told me that they felt as if they were constantly walking around on eggshells waiting for the next meltdown.

It was early July, and Christopher had only recently started the Friendly Group when I received an email from his mother, telling me he had broken his arm. She said that while Christopher was basically alright he was worried about getting the arm knocked by the other children. In fact what happened in the group was that he received a lot of attention and caring support in which he revelled. The problems only emerged some weeks later when the supporting cast and sling were removed and Christopher had been advised to 'use' his arm again. He was terrified and simply held his arm as if it was still in his sling, scared stiff to straighten it or use it, in case it snapped. It was as if his mental and emotional rigidity was being expressed in his physical body. In order to heal he had to trust. The Friendly Group offered a place of safety for him to begin to dip his toes into the pool of trust. His mother reported that Christopher had told her he had never felt so relaxed with other children. He felt they understood him; they 'got' his jokes; they liked his story ideas and they appreciated his intelligence and general knowledge (he soaked up factual information like a sponge). The other children listened to Christopher, and took his worries seriously.

As the group cohesion grew, so Christopher loosened up and began to trust that his arm could be strong again.

Fourteen months later - September

SESSION 1

The summer holidays were over and it was the start of new academic year. Christopher was now nearly 12. Much to everyone's surprise he arrived in a wheelchair. He gingerly stood up as he reached the entrance, and with the aid of crutches, made his way slowly into the group room where he sat on one chair with his right leg raised on another chair. The other children were eager to hear what had happened to Christopher. When he spoke, they all gazed up at him from their seated places on the floor cushions as he gave his story. He didn't begin with why he was sitting on the chair, eager as he was to tell the others about his summer trip first, but as the story developed, so did the story about why he had arrived in a wheelchair.

> *"I don't know if you remember last summer that my knee was a bit sore?"*
> he began. Several of the group nodded. They had remembered.
> *"Well on holiday, the pain got worse and worse and my knee has swollen right up. I can't bend it very well and it hurts to walk. I've been to the hospital for tests because no-one knows what it is."*

Christopher said no more and the session continued. A little later the children were invited to share their worries using the *Worry Bear*. Christopher then lent forward with a gesture that indicated that he wanted a turn.

> *"No-one knows what's wrong, but I'm worried that I'm going to break my leg and it's going to fall off,"* he said.
> *"Don't worry!"* interrupted Alicia, *"It will all be OK."*

I wondered if Alicia's instant reassurance was a way of defending against her own anxieties about her sick brother, who at the time was undergoing chemotherapy treatment for cancer. For her it was probably unthinkable to imagine anything terrible happening to Christopher in the same way as she couldn't bear to think about her brother not recovering. Christopher then continued.

"I've been to the hospital for lots of blood tests. It's so scary and I hate it because it hurts so much. They keep sticking these enormous needles into me. But I'm still going to school and everyone is being very nice about me being in a wheelchair. It's actually quite fun being in a wheelchair."

Christopher swung from pain to pleasure with the innocent straightforwardness of a child. The other children listened, their curiosity satisfied and the session continued.

One week later
SESSION 2 CHRISTOPHER BREAKS THE NEWS

The session started just like the previous week. The children played or chatted together before sitting on their cushions in the circle. This week the group was ready for Christopher and he duly took his throne-like position in one corner of the room, carefully placing his crutches out of the way as he gingerly raised his right leg on the second chair.

Trevor was the first to speak with the stone, eager to share his news about a recent gift of some Star Wars Lego. Yasir followed, describing in detail a computer game that he was currently enjoying. Christopher was the third to speak. He took the stone, handling it carefully and cradling it almost lovingly, as he cupped both hands together. The stone was his anchor. Each week when children hold the stone, it is like a trigger that centres and calms them, rather like a sound mantra is used for meditation. They become quickly and mindfully present and alert. I see it week after week and marvel at the way a simple pebble can have this effect, but it does.

"My leg has been hurting a lot," he said, looking around at the assembled faces.

"The doctors have found out what is wrong. It is cancer. I have a type of

bone cancer in my knee. That's why my knee looks swollen. It's a cancerous lump. I have to take lots of disgusting medicine. And they put this tube up my arm on Tuesday."

"I know what cancer is," interrupted Alicia, like she did the previous week. We let her continue. She needed to speak. The others remained silent.

"In your body you have two types of cells. You have normal cells and you have cancer cells. The cancer cells are different and they grow a lot and they grow fast. You can solve it with chemotherapy. My brother has cancer but he's getting better now. But the trouble is that the chemotherapy kills the good cells as well as the bad cells so you feel poorly. My brother was very poorly for a long time."

"Yes!" added Christopher. *"That's what I have got to have and the doctors told me I would feel poorly and they've said the treatment is going to last for nine months. That's an awfully long time."*

When you are 11, nine months really is an awfully long time. In fact it probably seemed to him to be an interminable length of time. Christopher was going to have treatment through the changing seasons, during Christmas, his birthday, Easter, for the whole of the school year. It was unimaginable to Christopher, but what this would mean to the whole family was unimaginable too.

"I know about cancer too," began Yasir (10).

Yasir explained about the division of cells and how cancer cells divide faster. He used his fingers to illustrate Christopher's legs in his explanations. He was completely matter-of-fact, speaking in a tone of voice that betrayed no emotion. Stick to the facts! Stick to the facts! You can control facts. You can understand facts. You can keep unwanted and troubling emotions at bay with facts. That is how the children often manage their anxiety about uncertainty. They immerse themselves in facts. Facts can be soothing and uncomplicated. They are definite and precise. They seem tangible and certain.

I wondered too, whether these matter-of-fact statements and questions were a defence against thinking the unthinkable, that Christopher could die. Or were they examples of the autistic fragmented way of thinking? It didn't matter. What mattered was that the children were able to acknowledge and share in Christopher's plight. They were prepared to think, to show interest and in a rather beautiful way, 'hold' Christopher. There was a strangely powerful energy in the room. Jeremy was next in the group to speak.

> *"I feel sorry for Christopher,"* he began. *"I went to the air show in the summer and I saw you there, Christopher. You looked OK then."* Then almost without a pause, Jeremy went on to say, *"I've got a 3D card here. Do you want to look at it?"* The card was passed round.

A feeling of normality was being resumed. The children talked of other things like computer games, homework and plans for the weekend. However it was important that Jeremy had been able to say he felt sorry. He spoke for the whole group, for on that day none of the others could actually voice those feelings. My colleagues and I did, though. We acknowledged that Christopher's news was a shock, that he was being very brave and that we would support him over the coming weeks and months

After the families and then my colleagues had left at the end of the second session, I wrote some notes. I needed to find a way to process this shocking news. Writing down my thoughts later that day helped me. I needed to reconnect with the side of myself that knew I had done the best I could that morning. These are the notes.

> *I somehow feel sick at the end of this session. Christopher told the group today about having cancer - he was worried beforehand about telling the group in case he might upset anyone - he was thinking of others more than himself. And the experts say that children with Asperger's don't have empathy! Well, Christopher had! His mother Karen rang me to tell me the news just before the children started arriving. She asked what I thought of Christopher sharing this news with the other children. She was matter-of-fact (holding it together, I suppose) and I reassured her that it would be good for Christopher and the other children.*
>
> *I hope it helped him to talk. Yasir and Alicia gave descriptions of what cancer is ... about cells dividing up. No-one mentioned you can die from cancer. How does one respond to this news?*
>
> *When the parents arrived they were in good spirits in anticipation of their usual coffee together while the children were in the session. Karen arrived last. At the end, when I went out ahead of the children to welcome the returning parents I was met with a rather subdued and slightly awkward group. I felt I couldn't say anything until I was sure Karen had spoken to them (even though their body language said it all). So I was probably coming across as rather awkward myself.*
>
> *I am now wondering how I behaved towards the children. Did I handle the situation well enough? Could I have done more? I don't know. But I did the best I could. I must remind myself of that, and my colleagues were wonderful.*

A month later, at an evening parents' session, some of the parents described the shock, distress and bewilderment expressed by their children on the way home that day.

The Following Week

SESSION 3

The children arrived in dribs and drabs. Christopher was the last to arrive and once again sat on the chair with his right leg supported. He seemed more agitated this week. The first five children shared their news, thoughts and feelings. It was now Christopher's turn.

> *"I was in hospital from Tuesday to Thursday,"* he began. *"They have to put in a line before they can start my treatment. They tried over and over again but they couldn't do it. It was so painful. Then they put me to sleep to do it but when I woke up they still hadn't got the tube in. My arm is really hurting now. I have to go to the hospital again on Monday and they are going to try again. The good thing though is that a friend came over for a sleepover yesterday and I've got another friend coming over today."*

The group listened to everything Christopher had to say; I noticed that he seemed angrier than usual. The next part of the session was with the *Bear Cards*.

> *"This week I would like to choose a Bear Card showing a bear which looks like how you are feeling about your parents at the moment,"* I said.

Christopher wanted to speak first. He had chosen two cards. One portrayed a very angry bear and one was of a happy bear. Prior to the session, Karen (Christopher's mother) had telephoned to let me know about the problems at the hospital and Christopher's associated anxieties. Christopher had told her that he realised that a delay in treatment could mean the cancer might spread and he could die. The fear of death is for most, the ultimate fear. Christopher had, however, found a way to express these fears openly with his mother. He felt safe with her. She had not 'fallen apart'. She was keeping strong for Christopher and knew that in order for him to cope with what was happening to him, he needed to know the facts about the cancer and the treatment, the steps along the way, and to some extent, the risks that went with them. This is what Christopher shared with his friends.

> *"I am angry and happy with my parents at the same time,"* he explained. *"They make me do horrible things and that is making me really angry with them. But they are being nice about it so I feel happy with them as well. But I'm really angry with my mum. She's asleep all the time. It makes me mad. But I'm thankful she's there though."*

Having the space to express this anger and frustration about his parents seemed to help Christopher. The other children had given him that space because they listened to what he said and responded without judgement. This was the pattern throughout this particular set of six sessions. In turn he was able to be playful and childlike and threw himself with enthusiasm into the *group story*. The story offers the children an opportunity to use their imaginations and communicate their hidden inner worlds in a safe and creative way. I have described this in more detail in Chapter 11. Here are some short extracts from the beginning of their story, where the children are deciding what to take on their journey quest. It is written here, just as it was typed and presented to the children.

```
Alicia is the first to speak.  She tells everyone that
she is going to take a magic lamp with her that has a
genie inside that can give us a million, billion wishes.
```

> *"You need to watch out!"* says Christopher, *"because genies can be crafty. You need to make sure that you wish for a lawyer to sort out the genie's mess when it happens!"* We all laugh at this idea.
> Later, Christopher shares what he would like to take.
> *"I want to take a super-powered wheelchair,"* says Christopher. *"It has super gadgets and it can fly and it is made out of solid gold."*
> We all look at the wheelchair and think it is brilliant. Alicia notices that the wheelchair even has arms that can do the cooking! This will be very useful as Jeremy has brought some delicious things for us to cook. The rest of the children give their ideas and Trevor is the last in the group to make his suggestion.
> Trevor tells us that he wants to take a very powerful computer that can plug into Christopher's wheelchair. He explains that it is as small as an iPod but it is as powerful as a 'Gray Super Computer'. It is shiny and black with an HD screen.

It's interesting that in the story Christopher acknowledged his physical difficulties; he wanted to be using a wheelchair but the fact it was made of gold and had special powers, speed and gadgets suggests that he felt empowered by his own wheelchair. There was optimism being expressed. However, his comments about sorting out the *"genie's mess"* might have been betraying his lack of trust about his health and life.

The story involved the children going on a quest to find treasure. Here is another extract from a later session.

"Wow!" cries Trevor, from high up in the air. *"I can see the treasure!"* *"Yes!"* agrees Alicia, *"The treasure is in a snake pit."*

We all land in the pit and Trevor swoops in to join us. Alicia's computer scans the pit to see if it's safe but discovers it's full of dangerous diamonds from outer space. Trevor leans forward and touches some of them then he fades into another dimension. Trevor has now disappeared. We've got to get him back! Christopher presses a button on his wheelchair and out pops a knife, which he uses to slash a new portal which creates an opening so that Trevor can manage to get back to us. But oh no! An enormous monster has followed him. It is in the shape of a cat with a big head but it has got seven eyes, eight tentacles, wings and three dinosaur heads coming out of its bottom. We need to escape! Jeremy grabs the treasure and we head off. We have to get through twenty dimensions and we need to travel clockwise but each dimension gets more dangerous.

We are under a mountain that is made of menozite and the portals to each dimension are activating the menozite. It's becoming radioactive and very dangerous. Christopher gets out some strong glue to seal up each of the portals as we go through. This deactivates the menozite. At last we are safe and Jeremy shows us the treasure.

I was curious about how the story takes the children to a snake pit; snakes can be seen as transformational symbols. The treasure is in a very dangerous place. They are also taken to different dimensions and the deeper they go the more dangerous it becomes. However, there's an order to it, and there is hope that they can come through it together, which they do. I wonder whether these dangers reflect, in a metaphorical way, the children's desires and fears about looking deep within themselves. It is frightening to think about death, loss and isolation, but the story provides a way of processing some of these fears in a safe way. The closing of the portals in the story is like the closing of the relational gaps between the children.

Indeed this group of children became very close during the year of Christopher's treatment. The parents also made a firm bond with each other and supported Karen during that year. On more than one occasion, when Christopher was undergoing chemotherapy and was at the risk of infection, other children from the group with minor colds were kept at home in order that Christopher would be able to attend. Given that for much of the year, he was unable to go to school, the Friendly Group became the one source of continued social contact outside of the home and hospital.

Christopher had a successful knee replacement and the cancer was completely removed. He is still in good health today. Christopher continued to be a member of the Friendly Group for another couple of years till he felt ready to leave.

POSTSCRIPT

About two years later when Christopher was 14, Romy, another boy of the same age who was fairly new to the group, wanted to share a worry. Romy didn't know about Christopher's medical history or year of treatments. In the first week that they met, Romy boasted a large scar on his leg following an injury sustained in a cycling accident. Christopher then trumped him with his knee scar, but Romy hadn't registered what Christopher told him about how he came to get it.

> "There's someone I've known for six years and he's been diagnosed with cancer. It's bone cancer and he only has three months to live. And he's my age," began Romy cautiously, looking around as if to gauge the others' responses. He wasn't looking at the adults. Christopher was quick with a response.
>
> "I expect he will go to the same hospital as me and see the same doctors, nurses and hospital teachers. I've been 'all clear' for two years now."
>
> Yasir then interjected with, "Well I hope with all my heart that he will get well again, Romy. I can't imagine what it would be like to lose someone close."

Two years earlier Yasir would have stuck to the facts; now he was reaching out to his new friend with an empathic response about another boy whom he didn't even know. Yasir had learnt so much about how to reflect on uncomfortable feelings through sharing Christopher's journey. He was able to respond from his sensitive side, and had become much more flexible and resilient. Deidre also could identify something of the sadness and worry felt by Romy and was able to show it when she said,

> "I hope he gets better too. I know what it was like to lose Granddad to cancer."
>
> "There's nothing you can really say at a time like this," commented Tom, who expressed what most of us were feeling. But Christopher wanted to say some more.
>
> "You should still meet up with your friend even if he is very ill and you should treat him like you always have done … you know, tease him and have a laugh … and not like he's made out of china or something fragile like that."

Christopher was clearly speaking from experience and his words and tone of voice seemed to touch the whole group. Illness doesn't need to make you a totally different person. Children are still children who want to have a joke and play. Through his illness Christopher learnt how to manage his anxieties better. In some ways, it was through the vulnerability of illness that Christopher discovered his inner strengths and became more tolerant and flexible. He also became a happier person and learnt how to enjoy life and to make successful friendships, even if he still struggled with his sensory issues. When he left the group a year later, this is what he said about the group at his last session:

> *"The Friendly Group has taught me how to be myself ... I can be me here ... but I feel happy and more confident at school now. I've made new friends and I know I don't have to 'put on a show' just to please other people."*

Christopher has grown up now and is a confident and healthy young man.

> **THINGS TO THINK ABOUT**
>
> I decided to include Christopher's story in this book for two reasons; one because it illustrates the resilience and strength a child can have in the face of adversity when he or she is well supported, and the second because I wanted you, the reader, to be inspired by the empathy that can be shown by children on the autism spectrum.
>
> I also wanted to show how children need to share feelings (just as much as adults) when they, or someone they know or care about, are faced with serious

illness. What comforts autistic children is to be clear about the facts of an illness and the treatments that are needed (timings and procedures). Of course every child is different and some children would not necessarily respond in the same way as Christopher and his group did. However, I would always give a group the opportunity to think and talk together about 'difficult things' (like illness, death or divorce) and support them in that process. The earlier chapters (such as 6, 7, 8 and 12) describe how to work with a group in the here-and-now, helping children to process their difficult feelings. This chapter illustrates the power of group process and how children can help each other. It can work in a family too.

Finally, it wasn't only Christopher who matured from this experience. All the children in his group did as well. And the parents gained a lot, not the least because Christopher's mother was able to share her journey with them. Christopher and his family were able to help each other and with the support of other key people in their lives, were also able to take advantage of what the Friendly Group had to offer.

Chapter 17

Beginnings in endings

It was an un-seasonally warm October morning and I was on my knees wiping dry the trampoline mat in readiness for the last session. The trampoline is always put away at the end of October because, during the winter months, even on a dry and sunny morning, like this one, the trampoline remains damp and slippery from the dew. However, I knew that it would be important for the children to be able to play on it today, because they wouldn't see it again until March. As I wiped the cloth back and forth over the wide expanse of the trampoline's black surface, I thought about how this was the end of the summer season and how the start of autumn was upon us.

It was also Nathaniel's 13th birthday that day.

"Oh dear!" exclaimed my colleague, Claire, *"I can see Nathaniel's mother coming up the path looking very worried."*

Sure enough, Faye could be seen purposefully heading towards us with a grim face. Behind her, Nathaniel followed, looking agitated and somewhat reluctant to come in. Faye was leading the way, holding a brightly coloured box in her hands, which she held out to me as if it was a peace offering.

"I'm so sorry. I'm so sorry," she repeated, *"Nathaniel's really cross with me. I've got this birthday cake for him and he says it is too babyish."*

In a flash I knew I had to act quickly.

> *"Let me take that from you,"* I offered as Faye handed over the box, *"And Nathaniel, come with me into the kitchen."*

Usually I provide a little cake for the children to share when it is a birthday. Nathaniel had already celebrated three previous birthdays in the group. However this time he had made a special request to bring his own cake as it was his 13th birthday and I had agreed. Claire and I let Faye know she could leave the cake with us and it would be alright. Then Nathaniel and I walked swiftly past the other children and into the kitchen; a private area that is usually considered out of bounds for the children. Nathaniel had difficulties with emotional regulation and I could feel he was about to have a 'meltdown'.

> *"I don't want that cake. Mum chose it and the box looks likes it's for a three-year-old,"* he began.
> *"I agree with you Nathaniel,"* I said, *"After all you have become a teenager today and this is a very babyish box, but let's look at the cake inside. It may be OK."* Nathaniel agreed and I could feel his tension diminishing as I opened the box.
> *"Well the cake looks delicious because it's made of chocolate and I know how much you like chocolate. I can see that the cake is in the shape of a caterpillar and I think it looks rather good."*
> *"It does look alright,"* said Nathaniel somewhat cautiously.

I knew that Nathaniel needed to feel more in charge of the situation, so I asked him if we should take the cake from the box and put it on a long plate. Would he like to add the candles himself? He took the spatula I offered and set to the task. I watched with baited breath as the cake nearly fell on the floor. It landed with a bit of a splat on the edge of the plate but I managed to straighten it without comment and it still appeared to be mainly intact. How interesting that he should be given a cake in the shape of a caterpillar. A caterpillar is a creature in a transitional state reminding me of Nathaniel, whose childhood was ending and adolescence just around the corner. In the same way that a caterpillar changes shape and eventually emerges from its cocoon stage as a fully formed butterfly, I had also noticed how Nathaniel had been changing both physically and emotionally in recent months. In just a few years he would be a young man. He began to put the blue and white candles onto his cake and soon the earlier reticence transformed into some enthusiasm.

> *"Can I eat the head?"* he asked eagerly, pointing out the piece of solid white chocolate in the shape of a head with facial features at one end.
> *"Of course you can, Nathaniel! It's your birthday after all,"* I replied.

There was then a little blip when Nathaniel snapped one of the candles by mistake. He hated to be clumsy, and in that second I could sense he was about to go on the defensive and could have given up. So with a magician-like sweep of the hand I replaced the broken candle saying, *"Here, Nathaniel, take this one! The chocolate is so thick that it makes it difficult to get the candles through, doesn't it?"* The offering was accepted as part of a seamless series of movements and he successfully finished the task to his satisfaction before we returned to the group room to begin the session.

Just before the start of *choosing time,* a tablecloth was spread out in the middle of the circle and Nathaniel's cake was brought in along with other snack foods and drinks. Nathaniel then asked to light his own candles and one by one we counted till we reached 13. The group sang '*Happy Birthday*' and Nathaniel blew out his candles before cutting the cake and making a wish. The cake was shared with the whole group. All very normal and familiar.

This ritual of celebrating a birthday has become an important part of the Friendly Group. It acknowledges both an ending and a beginning. The joint act of celebration further serves to create both bonds and memories for the group.

The importance of ritual

It's really important that an ending is properly recognised. When we are ready for a transition, it feels good to move on. Our journey through life is a constant cycle of beginnings and endings and it's how these times of transition are experienced that can determine how bumpy or smooth the road will be. Endings, and thus the new beginnings that follow, focus our attention.

Endings are not the end. They are transitions and people from across the world have developed their own rituals to mark particular transitions. Rituals allow people to come together and connections to be felt and made. Emotions can be expressed and released. Grief and joy, sadness and hope can intermingle. A parent might shed tears at their child's wedding, marking the end of childhood and the beckoning of this particular form of adulthood, moving from one kind of attachment to another. 11-year-olds weep and cheer as they write their signatures on school shirts on their last day in primary school. 16 and 18-year-olds dress up in their best clothes for their school prom after finishing their public exams.

Rituals allow the opportunity for memories to be recalled: the remembering serves to 'round things off'. Transitions are more bearable when memories are threaded into a narrative, and we have a place in that narrative. Telling the story of events and experiences anchors us in place and time and gives order and meaning; the experiences are bought alive once more and reinforce our sense of being within those remembered times. It's often the triumph over hardship and the achievement following effort that brings the greatest meaning to life. No wonder speeches celebrating such moments are made at weddings, anniversaries, funerals, festivals, jubilees and other ceremonies.

Rituals allow us to celebrate and to express and share our feelings with others. The honesty and intensity of expression, whatever its form, whether it is words, dance, music or feasting expresses and creates a bond with our fellow human beings. To be part of a ritual can give us an experience of being part of something greater than just ourselves.

Throughout the earlier chapters of the book there are stories of how the children in the Friendly Group cope with endings and beginnings. At the end of the sessions the simple rituals of the *Circle Time* and the *lighthouse goodbye* help the children to give meaning to their experience and to round the session off in preparation for going home.

Each term the children have to finish after their block of sessions and then re-start the group the following term. For the last session (of a six week block) we often create little ritual celebrations like having extra refreshments, playing a board game together and going around the circle sharing memories of that particular term. It helps the children to bond more and for the groups to continue to grow and mature.

Saying goodbye to childhood

SEAN'S STORY

When I first met Sean he was 12 and preparing for the transition from preparatory school to senior school. This was not the first transition between schools as his family had lived abroad and he had attended schools in two other countries before coming to the UK when he was ten. However this time, there were exams to be faced and although Sean had the academic ability he was struggling emotionally and was prone to unpredictable and angry outbursts. He quickly became overwhelmed in social company or when his routines were upset, and tended to either lash out or withdraw. These defensive behaviours often took no account of others and afterwards he would feel terribly remorseful, reigniting his anxiety yet further. He avoided the company of other children as a way of coping and was in danger of completely isolating himself.

> *"If I keep away from others I won't get into trouble,"* he would tell his parents, deciding that avoidance was the best course of action.
> *"I only want you to be happy,"* he told his mother time and time again.

Soon after Sean had joined the group I received an email that his mother had forwarded from his new school. Here is part of it.

```
"On Wednesday Mrs C. gave Sean a 'demerit' for being
'out of bounds'.  He then tore down her wall display and
she was very upset.  Yesterday on the visit to another
school for a science lecture, he had to be stopped
from crawling under the chairs in the auditorium.
Furthermore, yesterday there was an incident with some
Year 4 boys in the playground …"
```

Sean's mother felt at a loss to know what to do. She felt the tone of the email was blaming her; that she was in some way responsible for his behaviour. Many parents experience this. However, the email only reflected the teacher's feelings of helplessness, confusion and frustration. Sean acted out his feelings but was unable to talk about them. He hadn't been able to talk about his feelings in the group and couldn't talk about them at home either.

So his mother and I arranged for him to come and see me for a family session with her. From time to time, I meet with children outside the group. These sessions can offer a space for a family to feel supported together. After the session Sean's mother told me it had been a relief to not only see Sean relax, but to also hear him being able to acknowledge that he was finding life in his new school difficult.

However, as Sean settled into the group, his reticence to share feelings continued. Instead he took on the roles of the conciliator and the storyteller. If the group was feeling flat he would bring it to life with an amusing personal story. If the group was getting over-excited and a particular member was finding it too much, Sean would be the first to notice this and say something to calm the atmosphere and include that member of the group. Indeed Sean was always seeking practical ways to bring the group together and make it work, when it was in danger of fragmenting. He was the one who would remember the personal stories of others and ask them for updates. He never criticised others.

These behaviours, while charming and delightful on the surface, also suggested defensiveness against opening up and facing his inner turbulence. His stories seemed to be more as an entertainment to keep others at bay rather than as a means of making connections. During the less structured part of the sessions, he tended to be on the fringes, preferring to talk with one of the adults instead of joining in the group banter or play. However, Sean's family reported that he was beginning to make friends at school and seemed happier at home.

Three years later, during the winter before Sean was due to leave the group (and during a period in the gap between group sessions), Sean's mother, Ruth telephoned me.

"Anita, can you help me? I don't know what to do. I am so worried about Sean. He says he isn't worried about his GCSE's coming up in the summer but those terrible behaviours we saw three years ago are all coming

back. It's as if he's depressed. He says that he's not interested in anything anymore. We can barely get him out of the house to join us when we do things as a family. He isn't doing anything outside school now. He seems to have gone right back," said Ruth.

After listening to Ruth I offered to see Sean on his own, if he agreed. At 15 I felt it would be better if he saw me without his mother. Sean agreed to the plan and he came the following week. It was a familiar sight to see his tall thin body come into the room with that smooth gliding movement, then elegantly drop down on the settee opposite me. What was unfamiliar, were the tears.

Now he sat in front of me and wept. I passed him the box of tissues and he pulled out handfuls, taking off his spectacles to dab his wet and reddening eyes. It was as if he had let go enough to feel his feelings. Sean's emotions were usually hidden, couched in his stories. As he sat before me that day he had no story to tell; his emotions were gushing like a burst dam. So I sat quietly and didn't try to stem the flow. I could tell something very significant was happening before my eyes. He wept for several minutes and when he began to speak, he wasn't talking about exam stress. What he was talking about was far more deep rooted. He was struggling to find the words to express that existential angst of a teenager leaving childhood behind and moving into adolescence. Something was coming to an end and he was feeling the pain of loss, but he didn't know how to navigate his way towards this new beginning. After a while the words began to flow.

> *"I know it is about growing up,"* he said, *"But I don't get excited, worried or annoyed about things like I used to. I don't know what to do about it. There is a kind of emptiness inside me and it all feels so pointless."*
> *"Yes, it's very difficult when you have those feelings,"* I acknowledged.

> *"I used to get angry with my brother over sharing toys, but I don't even do that now because I'm not really interested in those toys anymore. How strange to feel sad about not fighting with my brother,"* he continued.
>
> *"It does feel sad when you no longer get the same pleasure out of toys you enjoyed as a child. And it's difficult when your relationship changes with a brother even if you were fighting. At least you were fighting together,"* I agreed, acknowledging the feelings he was expressing with the same kind of language. He was feeling the sadness as he spoke with a full heart.
>
> *"When I've got schoolwork to do, it feels better. Some people hate schoolwork, but for me it's a distraction from these sad feelings and thoughts. I like reading and there is a lot for me to read,"* he continued.
>
> *"So you are discovering that you enjoy your schoolwork more than playing with your old toys and games. Your reading and learning is giving you more pleasure,"* I added.
>
> *"Yes, I love learning languages too. Did you know that I have been teaching myself Swedish since we went on holiday to Sweden?"* he said.

Sean replaced his spectacles and looked at me, his tearful state being steadily replaced with a more peaceful calm. His passion had been spent. Two weeks later Sean was back in the group. He never mentioned the session we had together (just a nod of the head to acknowledge it on his arrival) but for the first time began to share some of his feelings in the group. He was able to share with the others how he found his old toys babyish and discovered he wasn't alone in this. He was like them; he had begun to connect with them at last. Banter was exchanged over which toys were still worth playing with. Group jokes emerged and reinforced the group cohesiveness. In addition, Sean enjoyed sharing his new teenage interests with the rest of the group and discovered there were others who shared some of them.

Preparing for an ending

From the very first day of starting the Friendly Group my role is not only to help the children to learn and to develop but also to prepare them to leave. For some children, their time in the group lasts for a year, for others it can be four or five years: but eventually the time comes when they will all leave the group. I've already discussed how children on the autism spectrum struggle with transition in Chapter 14, dealing with ending one thing and beginning something else.

As the Friendly Group runs in six week blocks of sessions, the start of each term offers a new beginning and the end of each term provides the experience of an ending. During week five of each of the six week blocks, the children are given the opportunity to express how they feel about the end of the sessions coming up. Beginnings and endings are played out time and time again.

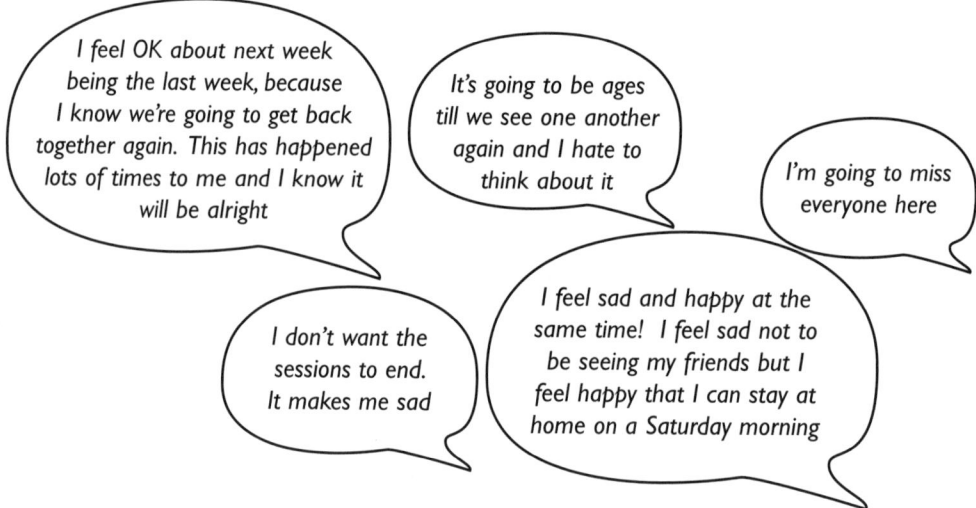

These are the sentiments usually shared in the group. The children hear that others feel the same as them; that they're not alone in having mixed feelings and that the group means something to them. They are given the opportunity to feel the sadness and the loss and to talk about it. Often memories are shared and the group cohesiveness is strengthened.

What I also find interesting is that when children know that they are going to leave in two or three months' time, they often 'step up to the plate' as it were, and begin to work and develop at an accelerated pace. It's as if the prospect of the ending triggers an inner urgency to reach out and engage.

A GOOD ENDING

It was the last term for Donald and Marc. They were both 16 and over the years had become good friends. They had been members of the group for eight years and they knew they were holding a record for the longest standing members. Each of them had been preparing for leaving for the past nine months and would bring it up from time to time in the group. Sometimes they mentioned it with light-heartedness, at other times they told the group they didn't want to think about having to leave. Their parents were also expressing regrets about the group coming to an end. It had been a part of their lives for such a long time. Other members of the group talked of their feelings of sadness about these two leaving. They were the 'group elders,' and the others looked up to them.

During this last set of sessions there had been opportunities for the two boys to talk about their future plans for college the following year, their early memories of being in the group and their recognition of how they had changed. Earlier in the term Marc had said,

> *"I can't believe I've been in the Friendly Group for eight years! That's half my life. When I started I didn't interact with people. But in the Friendly Group I've become a more socially competent person."*

Using this formal type of language is typical of autistic children; they either copy the language of the adults or create their own ways of expressing themselves. Donald had said in an earlier session,

> *"What I like about the Friendly Group is that we are here to share our worries and that we can make friends with people. It has worked for me."*

When we prepared the group in 'week five' for the last session the following week, others had said,

> *"I feel bittersweet. I'm sad Marc and Donald are leaving but I'm pleased they are moving on to new things."*
> *"I feel sad that two people are leaving. I will miss them."*
> *"I feel super sad today thinking about two of my favourite people leaving. They have always been in the group since I started and I wonder what it will be like without them."*

This is what Marc had to say;

> *"I know we have been talking about it but I feel a kind of shock to the system and feel really sad next week will be my last. But I'm feeling positive and open to new experiences."*
> *"And I am looking forward to the party next week,"* added Donald.

Whenever a child leaves there is the ritual of sharing party food and drinks, the giving of a card signed by everyone in the group, as well as a small gift of a mug. The child who is leaving is given a chance to say what has been important to them, what they have learned and what they have enjoyed. The newer members are given a role model of optimism and hope for their own future departure. There is also the opportunity at the very end of the session for each child to say what they have appreciated about having the 'leaver' in the group, what they like about that person and what that person has given to the group. The leavers hear positive affirmations from the others. Sometimes children do not know what to say other than something as simple as *"You are brilliant!"* or *"I liked playing on the trampoline with you"* or *"You always gave good ideas in the story"*. Other children remember certain significant experiences and others express appreciation about the way the 'leaver' has helped them or befriended them.

The ending becomes a celebration for the whole group. The qualities of the group as a whole are acknowledged and appreciated. The connections between them are deeply felt. They have had an experience of being a 'part' of something. When someone leaves it marks a new beginning as the next term there will be a new member starting. This group then becomes a new group with its own beginnings once again. When a new member starts it gives the rest of the group a chance to revisit the experience of when they were new, and sparks off a new group feeling for everyone.

> **THINGS TO THINK ABOUT**
>
> In this chapter I have described the particular rituals of the Friendly Group and told stories of children I have worked with. But endings such as these are important for all groups and all people, whether their group is a social, musical, workplace, community, sporting, academic or religious one. There truly are beginnings in endings.
>
> Whether you are a parent of a child or a professional working with a child or a group of children or young people, it's worth reflecting on how you celebrate endings, smoothing the way for new beginnings. Autistic children need clear rituals to mark transitions, but enjoy doing them 'your' way with them. You might like to invite them to create ending rituals with you.

Finally

And now you, the reader, are approaching the end of this book. Unlike a novel, there is no satisfying resolution of all the puzzles, no neat tying up of the loose ends. Instead, I hope that I leave you feeling energised and inspired about your own new beginnings.

I wonder, as a result of finishing this book, what your next beginning might be? Maybe you will have the confidence to try running a group of your own? Maybe you will discover new ways to communicate with your children, families and colleagues and maybe you will feel more hopeful that there is a positive future for your child, or a child you work with? I hope so!

And maybe you will go back and re-read passages in the book that you have found helpful, and discover new things second or third time around. Whatever your new beginnings are, have faith in the children you work or live with that they will blossom. And they will.

Appendix

Further openings for use with the *Bear Cards*

Pick up a bear who looks like you feel:
- Today
- About school at the moment
- About the Friendly Group at the moment
- When someone is unkind to you or unkind to someone else you know
- When someone asks you to do something you don't want to do
- When your parents ask you to do something you don't want to do
- When someone in the group is behaving in a way you don't like
- About going to a new school and leaving an old one
- About going into a different Friendly Group
- About leaving the Friendly Group / about 'so and so' leaving the Friendly Group
- When a grown up asks you to share your worries
- If someone in the group feels sad or cross
- About having Asperger's Syndrome or autism
- About being taken seriously in the Friendly Group
- When someone listens to you and takes you seriously
- When someone is not listening to you
- About this/next week being the last week of the term
- When a parent does not listen to you or understand you
- When a parent does not take seriously something that is important to you
- When something bad has happened (like you've been in a fight, lost something or felt frightened)
- When you are put under pressure
- If you feel forced to do something
- When a grown-up asks you to do something without warning
- About how a friend is treating you at the moment
- When a brother/sister/cousin troubles or annoys you
- About having pocket money or not and if you are, how you are allowed to use it
- When you heard about (another person's) worry in the group last week
- When you are being laughed at or teased
- If you were told you couldn't use your phone or other technology anymore
- About having a visitor today
- About a family member you know, who has died - if that hasn't happened to you, imagine how you might feel
- When something goes wrong

Bear Cards can be obtained through Amazon and other good suppliers
Veeken, J. (2012) *The Bear Cards: Feelings Q Cards* 2nd Edn

References and further reading

Alvarez, A. (1992) *Live Company: Psychoanalytic psychotherapy with autistic, borderline, deprived and abused children* London: Routledge
Attwood, T. (1998) *Asperger's Syndrome: A guide for parents and professionals* London: Jessica Kingsley
Attwood, T. (2008) *The Complete Guide to Asperger's Syndrome* London: Jessica Kingsley

Bettelheim, B. (1978) *The Uses of Enchantment: The meaning and importance of fairy tales* London: Peregrine
Bion, W. (1984) *Learning from Experience* London: Maresfield
Bollas, C. (1987) *The Shadow of the Object: Psychoanalysis of the unthought known* London: Free Association Press
Bowlby, J. (1969) *Vol 1: Attachment* London: Pelican
Buzan, T. (2001) *Head Strong: How to Get Physically and Mentally Fit; Powerful principles to develop your mind/body connection* London: Thorsons
Buzan, T. with Buzan, B. (2000) *The Mind Map Book* London: BBC Worldwide

Casement, P. (1985) *On Learning from the Patient* London: Tavistock
Cattanach, A. (1997) *Children's Stories in Play Therapy* London: Jessica Kingsley
Copley, B. & Forryan B. (1997) *Therapeutic Work with Children and Young People* London: Cassell
Cotugno, A. J. (2009) *Group Interventions for Children with Autism Spectrum Disorders* London: Jessica Kingsley Publishers
Cotugno, A.J. (2011) *Making Sense of Social Situations: How to run a group-based intervention program for children with Autism Spectrum Disorders* London: Jessica Kingsley Publishers

Foulkes, S.H. (1984) *Theraputic Group Analysis* London: Karnac Books Ltd
Frith, U. (2003) *Autism: Explaining the Enigma* (2nd Ed) Oxford: Wiley
Frith, U. (2014) Autism - Are We Any Closer to Explaining the Enigma? *The Psychologist* Vol 27 No 10 pp.744-745

Gerhardt, S. (2004) *Why Love Matters: How affection shapes a baby's brain* Hove, Sussex: Bruner-Routledge

Grandin, T. (2006) *Thinking in pictures* London: Bloomsbury

Grotjahn, M. (1993) *The Art and Technique of Analytic Group Therapy* London: Jason Aronson Inc,

Haddon, M. (2003) *The Curious Incident of the Dog in Night-time* London: Jonathan Cape

Hogan, J. M. (1968) *Impelled Into Experiences: The story of the outward bound schools* UK: Educational Productions

Jaffe, A. Symbolism in the Visual Arts in **Jung, C**. (1978) *Man and his Symbols* London: Picador

Johnson, R.A. (1993) *Owning Your Own Shadow: Understanding the dark side of the psyche* San Francisco: *Harper*

Kaufman, B.N. (1994) *Son Rise: The miracle continues* Tiburon, California: H J Kramer Inc

Kaufman, G. (1992) *Shame: The power of caring* (3rd Ed) Schenkman Books, Inc. Rochester, Vermont

Moran, H. (2010) Clinical observations of the differences between children on the autism spectrum and those with attachment problems: The Coventry Grid *Good Autism Practice*, 11/2 2010

Nitsun, M. (1996) *The Anti-Group: Destructive forces and their creative potential* London: Routledge

Pinkola Estes, C. (1993) *Women Who Run With Wolves: Contacting the power of the wild woman* London: Rider

Rogers, C. (2003) *Client Centred Therapy* (new Ed) London: Constable & Company Ltd

Sacks, O. (1973) *Awakenings* London: Duckworth

Sacks, O. (1985) *The Man who Mistook his Wife for a Hat* London: Picador

Schore, A. N. (2003) *Affect Dysregulation and Disorders of the Self* New York: Norton

Schore, A.N. (2001) Effects of a secure attachment on right brain development, affect regulation and infant health *Infant Mental Health Journal 2*

Sunderland, M. (2000) *Using Storytelling as a Therapeutic Tool with Children* Bicester: Speechmark

Tustin, F. (1986) *Autistic Barriers in Neurotic Patients* London: Karnac Books Ltd

von Franz, M.L. The Process of Individuation in **Jung, C.** (1978) *Man and his Symbols* London: Picador

Waters, T. (2004) *Therapeutic Storywriting: A practical guide to developing emotional literacy in primary schools* London: David Fulton
White, M. (2009) *Magic Circles: Self-esteem for everyone in Circle Time* (2nd Ed) London: Sage
Williams, D. (1992) *Nobody Nowhere* Canada: Doubleday
Wing, L. (1996) *The Autism Spectrum: A guide for parents and professionals* London: Constable
Wing, L. & Gould, J. (1979) Severe Impairments of Social Interaction and Associated Abnormalities in Children: Epidemiology and classification *Journal of Autism and Developmental Disorders*, 9, pp.11-29
Winnicott, D.W. (1964) *The Child, the Family and the Outside World* London: Pelican
Winnicott, D.W. (1965) *The Maturational Processes and the Facilitating Environment* London: Hogarth Press and the Institute of Psychoanalysis
Winnicott, D.W. (1985) *Playing and Reality* London: Pelican

Yalom, Irvin D. with Leszcz, M. (2005) *The Theory and Practice of Group Psychotherapy* (5th Ed) New York: Basic Books